PROVISIONAL CONCLUSIONS

A Selection of the Poetry of Eugenio Montale

Eugenio Montale

Translated by Edith Farnsworth

HENRY REGNERY COMPANY *Chicago*

Manufactured in the United States of America
Published by Henry Regnery Company
180 North Michigan Avenue
Chicago, Illinois 60601
Library of Congress Catalog Card Number: 72-126149
International Standard Book Number: 0-8092-8039-6

PROVISIONAL CONCLUSIONS

Preface

THE STAR of Eugenio Montale has been late and long in rising in the firmament of international letters. This is to be accounted for not only by the fact that the Italian language is perhaps less familiar to foreigners than is French but also by the great cataclysms, the world wars, the social upheavals, and the political misfortunes and disgraces that disturbed and deformed the western continents during the youth and early maturity of the poet and inhibited the diffusion of Italian art over the Alps and across the Atlantic. Then, too, the poetry of Montale, although it reflects the events from which it springs, rarely makes direct reference to them, and the resulting effect of aloofness has led to the epithet "hermetic." Thus, even Italian readers have been rather too easily convinced that Montale could not be categorized and would not be understood.

So the poems came out in part and parcel, beginning with *Cuttlefish Bones*, first published by Gobetti in 1925, and it has remained for Mondadori to close the long time intervals and impart a certain unity to the basic works by presenting *Cuttlefish Bones* (1948), *Occasions* (1949), and *The Storm and Other Poems* (1957) in uniform volumes. Translations have now appeared in various languages. Among these translations are excellent French translations of all three volumes (Gallimard, 1966), the selected poems translated into English by George Kay and published by the University of Edinburgh in 1965, and the American edition, also of selected poems, brought out in 1966 by New Directions.

A substantial volume of critical and interpretative material has also appeared, and profound attention has been given to a poetic personality whose very elusiveness is provocative.[1] Not only have conventional

---

[1] *See*, for instance: Emilio Cecchi; "Alla ricerca della gioventù," *Il Secolo* (Oct. 31, 1925); Sergio Solmi: "Scrittori negli anni," Milan, *Il Saggiatore* (1963), pp. 19-21; Gianfranco Contini: "Dagli Ossi alle Occasioni," in *Esercizi di lettura* (Florence: Le Monnier, 1947); Carlo Bo: "Della poesia di Montale," in *Otto studi*, (Florence: Valecchi, 1939); Francesco Flora: "Eugenio Montale," in *Scrittori contemporanei* (Pisa: Nistri-Lischi, 1952) Gianfranco Contini: "Montale e la bufera," in *Letteratura* (1956): Pietro Bonfiglioli: "Da Pascoli a Montale," in *Studi per il*

scholarly labors been expended, but various modern techniques of analysis have been applied to the poetry and to the author as revealed, intimated, or even concealed in his works. Many of these studies are both interesting and apt; some of them reflect the siftings of correspondence between the poet and close friends. Out of these emerge details of personal experience that provide occasional explanations for allusions that are otherwise hopelessly dark, and this is doubtless gratifying to eyes that scan the verse with the honest desire to read and to understand. But the springboard does not measure the jump and the diving board does not describe the grace and audacity of the dive, so it is perhaps fair to say that much of the critical material sheds little light upon the qualities and purposes of the verse it is trying to expound. Few disagree with Professor Rebay, who says he likes to know what he is reading about, and we may find ourselves illuminated when he gives us a key to "the theatricals of childhood" referred to in "Elegy of Pico Farnese." We know that Montale began the poem while spending a few days at the country estate of Tommaso Landolfi, and that there was an ancient hall on the property in which the family used to perform plays. But the light goes out almost instantly when we see the board but not the dive and note that our insight into the real content and purpose of the poem is hardly deepened at all. To know that Montale, like anybody else, spent weekends with his friends does not invite us to a deeper understanding of the real intent of the curiously fascinating poem that was the result of this particular visit.

To such an understanding Montale himself offers the best key in the collection of sketches written over a period of many years for the *Corriere della Sera* of Milan, later published under the title *La Farfalla di Dinard*. Here many impressions gained from unannotated references, such as to "a love of bearded women," may be tentatively corrected, and the reader, in this case, may give up the notion that allusion is being made to the witches in Macbeth and conclude that the poet was talking about a trusted family servant whom he knew as a boy. The passage, so corrected, would lead to an implication of attachment or loyalty to a childhood attendant and not to a suggestion of evil presage. *La Farfalla* contains many such hints and insights, and since the sketches were cre-

---

centenario della nascita di Giovanni Pascoli (Bologna Commissione per i testi di lingua, 1962), Vol. I, D'Arco Silvio Avalle: "Gli Orecchini di Montale," *Il Saggiatore* (1965); Silvio Ramat: *Montale* (Florence: Valecchi, 1965); Luigi Rosiello: "Analisi statistica della funzione poetica nella poesia montaliana," in *Struttura, uso e funzioni della lingua* (Florence: Valecchi, 1965).

ated to appear in the literary column of a daily newspaper, they are written with fluency and humor, providing an incomplete glossary of poetic images, quantitatively insufficient but still, where the item is included, certainly helpful.

If, on the other hand, Montale had written of all of his aesthetic experiences concomitantly in the *Corriere* for the daily readers of the literary page and in the volumes of his poems for the angels, we would still be required to read a great many books, and in a number of languages, if we wished to inform ourselves of the extensive background that provides sources, influences, and inspiration for an admittedly solitary life. Offering all three, and surely at the top of the list, is Dante. Here, easily traceable references are numerous; often they are imperative. For the translator they frequently pose a problem, as when their inclusion in identifiable form would lead to an expansion that would deform verse and stanza, and their omission would deprive the poem of the overtones and reverberations that belong to it. Thus, the word *vivagno*, if deprived of its Dantesque past, would emerge as "selvedge," coming as a shock in the Montalian context, whereas, admitting the Infernal origin, it could lead us all the way back to the *Veglio di Creta*, threatening the symmetry of the brief poem *"Il tuo volo"* ("Your Flight") as it appears in *The Storm*.

To attempt even a listing of sources and influences would be incautious. Nobody has read the same books as has even a close friend, and few of us have read even a small part of those which have left traces, large or small, in the poetry of Montale. From German literature, Goethe looms large and Hoelderlin perhaps even larger. From the French, Rimbaud, Baudelaire, Apollinaire, and probably many others. In Spanish, Don Quixote is surely not the only knight, and from English and American sources we can detect the presence of the centuries from Shakespeare to Eliot and from Melville and Emily Dickinson to Hemingway and Steinbeck. From the native terrain, not only Dante but Foscolo and Leopardi are present and living.

Much has been written about all these influences, to which the studious and the students can turn for discussion and elaboration. For the purposes of the present volume, such material would be superfluous and inappropriate; even Montale himself has added only the most infrequent and sketchy of notes, as in the case of "Park at Caserta," where for the reference to the Mothers who chafe their knuckles as they search for the void, he simply refers us to Goethe "for a rather inadequate explanation." I, therefore, have annotated only where such satire or colloquialism occurs that could not be understood by non-Italian readers. It is to be hoped that the translated poems will speak with their own voice, that is, the voice of poetry, and that they will convey not information but literary experience.

The stylistic traits of Montalian poetry contrast significantly, as has been noted, with those of his prose. Where the prose is the writing of a competent critic and journalist, clear and effective, endowed furthermore with its special charm and delicacy, the poems are illuminated and often clouded by apocalyptical intimations and situations that suggest that no reader is contemplated, possibly not even invited. Sometimes we have the impression of overhearing some murmured confession, which we do not make out entirely; often we find ourselves surrounded by landscapes composed of type elements—abstracted components, streams, grottoes, shores—before which Dantesque or sylvan backdrop a known and specific figure or element may appear or move, such as Duilio the boatman or the well-remembered spiral flight of stairs or prototypical items such as a scale, a hair, or a string. By this time the conundrum has become far-reaching, and the pack of the readers is apt to divide into those who think that no apocalypse was envisioned or intended and that Montale is quite "down to earth" and those who look for visions from every inch of earth.

The language of Montale is seen to undergo a long evolution from his earliest poems, which employ archaic words and usages in free combination with the immediacy of current speech, to those of the succeeding period, in which the antique heritage dies out in favor of the simplest of everyday parlance, intimate but never banal. From the beginning to the present, the play-on-words, the magic pun, the double sense turns up now and again and serves as a soundless pivot which turns from one image to another. Along with the language elements, the syntax becomes more compact as the years pass: the visions that formerly were introduced by protracted, Leopardian, and leisurely descriptions, leading in turn to a contemplative anecdote, fade not into the light of common day but into a kind of lantern or fire light, and with this the style may be seen to lose a certain characteristic unevenness that gave rise, on the one hand, to a tragic groping and, on the other, to poems of the greatest skill, power, and distinction, such as "News from Mount Amiata," "The Woodcock," and "Dream of the Prisoner."

As in the case of many great poets, the lyrical elements present in *Cuttlefish Bones* and developed with all the resources of terminal or internal rhyme, of meter and alliteration, tend to diminish in subsequent experience, to ripen, perhaps to harden a little, to become more intrinsically structured. The stricter rhyme schemes are left behind; the youthful fervor remains exalted, but it turns darker in tone as the impact symbolized by *The Storm* produces its bitter and lasting reaction. The quality of aloofness is in no way diminished; indeed, the symbols are rather more dense, more novel, and richer in their combinations and modulations, without a hint that the reader is any less the outsider than he was in the earliest poems. As an example take "In the Park at Caserta." The theme here is *object*: its presence falteringly illuminated by the sun, its reflections, its proliferation, differentiation (roots and stamens, both from an ultimate point), its threat of entrapment (liane, clutching unremittingly at the passerby), its labyrinthine menace (the sardonic monkey puzzle tree), as against the emerging "ten" of torches, spheres, or fingers that are to roughen their knuckles as they try to regain the serenity and wisdom of empty space. The Mothers are the Goethian figures that inhabit the void and hold the records and designs of life. By way of introduction and certainly not fortuitously, the cruel swan claims the reflecting surface of the pool and smoothes his plumage down, presumably composing in his cold, white breast all his legend of rape and abduction. The author here is no longer Hyperion, no longer the melancholy youth bewailing the loss of an Age of Gold. He is as silent and as revealing as the painter of a universal canvas. It may be that there are those to see, or perhaps there is no one at all. If we are there, on hand, we may be looking at the artist lost in the labyrinth, or it may be we who are lost and trapped and he who, with roughened knuckles, has regained the designs of the void.

Carrying forward for a moment the symbolic ten as the native or organic implementation of the human being in the tumult of life, let us examine a little more observantly the ten Montalian spheres, torches, or digits. Perhaps the first psychological trait that we should note is the infallible predilection for the small and the disavowal of the large. The only thing in Montale that is recorded as grandiose is the cloud appearing above the tombside on which the dead dog lies extended (*"Sarcophagi"*). The composition is always made up of the tiny, the unpretentious, the semi-abstraction, semi-concretion. Even if the poetic element chosen is very small indeed, still the poet prefers to avail himself of it in reflection rather than in primary image and the choice of mirrors forms one of the most original traits, varying, as it does, from the pool or the well to the soup ladle and the mollusc's valve.

With the reflection, the distortion soon follows: the stone breaks the pool's surface; the wind ruffles it; a breath blows the gentle magnolia into the background of the ladle's picture, in which the pointed muzzles of lost pets are reflected. The threat is there, extrinsic or intrinsic; rarely does a force act so benignly as to invoke the shelter of the magnolia for the faithful and the dead. Force, indeed, is the essence of the storm that drove the poet into seclusion and into some of his noblest poetry. If force is the measure of evil, the quality is filth as is stated quite overtly and furiously in the "Point Counterpoint" that we have placed at the end of the poems taken from *The Storm*.

Turning back to the object and the reflection, one notable example might be cited in which the face takes shadowy color as it rises from the cold depths of the water in the bucket ("The Windlass Squeaks . . .") and is shattered by the poet himself when he bends closer. Whose is the face that recoils, shatters, and grows old? Whether it is of a loved woman or whether it is the poet's own, thus converting the poem into an elegy for Narcissus, perhaps even Montale would not wish to guess. In any case, the significant fact is that the poet acted—and the aged and broken face was sent back by the ruthless module of the windlass, to humid darkness.

In this brief and rapt poem we perceive an expression having much to do with the passivity that is one of the determining characteristics of the poetry and of the poetic personality of Montale.

Since, also, reflections can be reduplicated, even proliferated and projected, as by the boy with the little mirror on the roof ("Day and Night"), and since this is not an organic plethora, as of the snap beans ("Eclogue"), but a mechanical process, once it leaves the soup ladle, open to ambiguous circumstances and forces, hence to mutations and even contradictions, misunderstandings and paradoxes might be expected—and indeed they occur:

> . . . And I recant
> under the power that weighs upon us all around
> I yield to the witchcraft of knowing of myself
> nothing that is outside myself; if I so much
> as raise my arm, the act
> is altered, it shatters on a looking-glass,
> its memory blanches, vanishes and the gesture
> now has naught to do with me,

> *(Two in the Twilight)*

So the world changes from a lost El Dorado, nostalgically dreamed of and devotedly evoked, to a "ricochet of rings," a tambourine at a tomb and the futility, even dangerousness, of any action is emphasized more and more. The paradox appears frequently, often with enormous effectiveness from the technical viewpoint, along with a sliding from one pan to the other of the always overpowering balance measuring despair. Note the last few lines of "The Balcony" for an illustration of the effect:

The life which glimmers dimly
is for your eyes alone to know,
and toward that twilight you lean out
from my unlighted window.

See the ricochet of rings, the subtle shift of dimly glimmering life from external to internal and then outward again, of eyes looking from outside inward before they alight like moths upon the poet's dark window and become "you" to lean out toward a light now cosmic and burning low.

These same verses also bring us to the great conundrum, namely, the "*tu,*" the "you," the inspiration at the same time of both poetry and life. "You" is one or it may be all; it is the companion, even though, as in the case of Dora Markus, it may be personally unknown. It is the creature, or the essence, to be adored, the loss of which is the most intolerable ("Motets"), and yet, although "you" elicits a high poetic intensity in many poems, it is hard to think of an example of a love poem in any previously accepted sense. And once in a while, by a fulminating ricochet, "you" becomes evil, as in the "Serenata Indiana." By another rebound of paradoxes "you" may become "I," to give the supplementary "*tu suis*" of the Rimbaudian "*je est.*"

These comments are not intended as other than a few scattered suggestions, in no way either complete or infallible, to help the English-speaking reader in a first or even subsequent approach to a poet who shows, in his disillusionment and alienation, all the characteristics of the truly contemporary artist. In Montale, however, to be essentially, solidly of our age does not imply the break in the continuity of history or the adoption of current jargons or badges of any description, and despite plainer talk, fewer literary allusions, and the use of very simple verse forms, despite recent poems that suggest that Montale is at last seeking understanding from his reading public—still he will probably remain as "hermetic" in his seventies as he was in his thirties, simply because to him the vision, and nothing else, is life and this is the case for only a few, if any, of his readers.

Included in the present volume are approximately sixty of the poems that are contained in the three Mondadori volumes, *Ossi di Seppia, Le*

Occasioni, and *La Bufera.* To these have been added "In the Void" (*"Nel Vuoto"*) written in 1924 and published in *Satura* in 1962, and "Point Counterpoint" (*"Botta e Risposta"*), written in 1962 and published in *Satura* the same year.

E. F.

Fiesole
April, 1970

Contents

CUTTLEFISH BONES

REJOICE IF THE WIND . . .

Rejoice if the wind which penetrates the orchard
should usher back to you the surge of life;
for the entangled memories,
left for running time to bury,
orchard it was not, but reliquary.

The sound you hear is not of wings in flight,
but stirrings of the eternal womb,
and you will see this fringe of solitary
soil assume a new gestation.

This side of the steep wall yonder there is turbulence
If you proceed, you may encounter
there the phantom which provides salvation;
for it is there that tales are woven
with ablated actions for the wager of the future.

Look for a broken mesh in the net
which holds us tight, jump out, escape!
I have been praying for your flight—now slight
will be my thirst, less bitter my frustration.

2

GODI SE IL VENTO . . .

Godi se il vento ch'entra nel pomario
vi rimena l'ondata della vita:
qui dove affonda un morto
viluppo di memorie,
orto non era, ma reliquiario.

Il frullo che tu senti non è un volo,
ma il commuoversi dell'eterno grembo;
vedi che si trasforma questo lembo
di terra solitario in un crogiuolo.

Un rovello è di qua dall'erto muro.
Se procedi t'imbatti
tu forse nel fantasma che ti salva:
si compongono qui le storie, gli atti
scancellati pel giuoco del futuro.

Cerca una maglia rotta nella rete
che ci stringe, tu balza fuori, fuggi!
Va, per te l'ho pregato,—ora la sete
mi sarà lieve, meno acre la ruggine . . .

ENGLISH HORN

The wind which plays attentively tonight
—reminiscent of the clash of tambourines—
the instruments of the tangled trees, and sweeps
the horizon with copper
where streaks of splendor fly
like kites in a resounding sky,
(Traveling clouds, bright realms
up there! Doors half ajar
of lofty Eldorados!)
and the sea which, scale by livid
scale, is changing color,
flinging down a gush
of convoluting foam;
if the wind, this evening, born and already
dying in a slowly darkening hour,
could tune the discordant counterpart,
your heart.

CORNO INGLESE

Il vento che stasera suona attento
—ricorda un forte scotere di lame—
gli strumenti dei fitti alberi e spazza
l'orizzonte di rame
dove strisce di luce si protendono
come aquiloni al cielo che rimbomba
(Nuvole in viaggio, chiari
reami di lassú! D'alti Eldoradi
malchiuse porte!)
e il mare che scaglia a scaglia,
livido, muta colore
lancia a terra una tromba
di schiume intorte;
il vento che nasce e muore
nell'ora che lenta s'annera
suonasse te pure stasera
scordato strumento,
cuore.

FALSETTO

Esterina, your twentieth year is threatening,
an ash-pink cloudbank, slowly lengthening,
to take you for its own.
You understand this, and you do not fear.
We shall see you soon enveloped
in a haze condensed or ripped
by heavy winds; then presently you will emerge,
sun-tanned by the surge of ash, your face
like the huntress Artemis, intent
upon adventure farther off.
Your twenty autumns mount,
clasped by your traversed springs,
there rings for you a carillon
of premonition from an Elysian sphere.
May no sound turn you into
a fissured urn; for you I pray
the harmony ineffable of tinkling bells.

You do not fear tomorrow's doubt.
Light of heart, you lie down on the rock
shining with brine and in the sun
you bronze your limbs, like the lizard
sleeping on the naked stone.
Youth implicates you in its lure
and grips you in a snare of grass.

FALSETTO

Esterina, i vent'anni ti minacciano,
grigiorosea nube
che a poco a poco in sé ti chiude.
Ciò intendi e non paventi.
Sommersa ti vedremo
nella fumea che il vento
lacera o addensa, violento.
Poi dal fiotto di cenere uscirai
adusta più che mai,
proteso a un'avventura più lontana
l'intento viso che assembra
l'arciera Diana.
Salgono i venti autunni,
t'avviluppano andate primavere:
ecco per te rintocca
un presagio nell'elisie sfere.
Un suono non ti renda
qual d'incrinata brocca
percossa!; io prego sia
per te concerto ineffabile
di sonagliere.

La dubbia dimane non t'impaura.
Leggiadra ti distendi
sullo scoglio lucente di sale
e al sole bruci le membra.
Ricordi la lucertola
ferma sul masso brullo;
te insidia giovinezza,

It is the water which inures you; in its depths
you find yourself renewed.
You dwell within it as a stone,
an alga, creature of a sea
whose salty tooth does not attack
but turns you shoreward, grown
more pure.

Be wise and do not dim the sunny day
with prescient whims. Challenge
the on-coming with your gaiety; your shrug
of shoulder razes to the ground the fortress
of your ominous future.
You rise and venture on the frail
footbridge which spans the whirling rapids:
etched is your profile on a ground of pearl.
You pause at the tremulous, topmost thwart
then, laughing, as if plucked
by the wind in sport, you fling yourself
into the clasping arms
of your celestial friend.

We shall be looking on, we of the race
that never leaves the earth.

quella il lacciòlo d'erba del fanciullo.
L'acqua è la forza che ti tempra,
nell'acqua ti ritrovi e ti rinnovi:
noi ti pensiamo come un'alga, un ciottolo,
come un'equorea creatura
che la salsedine non intacca
ma torna al lito piú pura.

Hai ben ragione tu! Non turbare
di ubbie il sorridente presente.
La tua gaiezza impegna già il futuro
ed un crollar di spalle
dirocca i fortilizi
del tuo domani oscuro.
T'alzi e t'avanzi sul ponticello
esiguo, sopra il gorgo che stride:
il tuo profilo s'incide
contro uno sfondo di perla.
Esiti a sommo del tremulo asse,
poi ridi, e come spiccata da un vento
t'abbatti fra le braccia
del tuo divino amico che t'afferra.

Ti guardiamo noi, della razza
di chi rimane a terra.

SARCOPHAGI

1

Where the girls with curling locks make their way,
bearing on their shoulders brimming amphoras
and stepping firmly with so light a tread;
and the opening of the valley down below
awaits them vainly,
where a pergola of vines shades its bed
and the hanging clusters sway.
The sun which to its zenith climbs,
the slopes partly glimpsed,
display no tints: in this bland minute,
mother, not step-parent,
stricken nature makes the swarms
of her blithe creatures gay
in wanton forms.
World which sleeps or world which glories
in unchanging being, who can say?
Oh passerby, do offer it
the best shoots from your orchard.
Then continue: in this valley
is no shifting dark and bright.
Your way will lead you far from here,
where you will find no hearthside light,
being too dead;
follow the ranging of your stars.
So farewell, youthful curling locks;
bearing the brimming amphoras, make your way.

SARCOFAGHI

1

Dove se ne vanno le ricciute donzelle
che recano le colme anfore su le spalle
ed hanno il fermo passo sí leggero;
e in fondo uno sbocco di valle
invano attende le belle
cui adombra una pergola di vigna
e i grappoli ne pendono oscillando.
Il sole che va in alto,
le intraviste pendici
non han tinte: nel blando
minuto la natura fulminata
atteggia le felici
sue creature, madre non matrigna,
in levità di forme.
Mondo che dorme o mondo che si gloria
d'immutata esistenza, chi può dire?,
uomo che passi, e tu dagli
il meglio ramicello del tuo orto.
Poi segui: in questa valle
non è vicenda bi buio e di luce.
Lungi di qui la tua via ti conduce,
non c'è asilo per te, sei troppo morto:
seguita il giro delle tue stelle.
E dunque addio, infanti ricciutelle,
portate le colme anfore su le spalle.

2

Wayfarer, now let your step
be warier: at a stone's throw
from here you will see
a rarer scene.
The door of a shrine, fast rusted,
is closed forever.
A vast light comes down
upon the threshold deep with grass encrusted.
And here where no human step will sound,
a lean cur keeps his vigil,
extended motionless upon the ground.
He sleeps, and never more will stir,
at this sultry hour.
Above the roof a grandiose
cloud appears.

3

The fire which crackles
on the hearth dies down
and a darkening air imposes
on a world irresolute. A tired old man
dozes by the fire-iron
in the sleep of the abandoned.
Do not awaken, sleeper, in this
unfathomable light that metal

2

Ora sia il tuo passo
piú cauto: a un tiro di sasso
di qui ti si prepara
una piú rara scena.
La porta corrosa d'un tempietto
è rinchiusa per sempre.
Una grande luce è diffusa
sull'erbosa soglia.
E qui dove peste umane
non suoneranno, o fittizia doglia,
vigila steso al suolo un magro cane.
Mai piú si muoverà
in quest'ora che s'indovina afosa.
Sopra il tetto s'affaccia
una nuvola grandiosa.

3

Il fuoco che scoppietta
nel caminetto verdeggia
e un'aria oscura grava
sopra un mondo indeciso. Un vecchio stanco
dorme accanto a un alare
il sonno dell'abbandonato.
In questa luce abissale
che finge il bronzo, non ti svegliare

simulates. And you who walk,
go slowly; throw first of all
a log upon the flame, a ripe pine cone
into the hamper in the corner.
To the floor there fall
provisions, which were set aside
for the final journey.

4

But where to seek the tomb
of the lover and of the faithful friend,
the beggar's grave and that of the young boy;
where to seek a sanctuary
for those who receive the ember
from the first flame;
oh, by a hint of peace, slight as a toy,
may the urn be decorated!
Leave the muted granite host
for the derelict slabs
which bear occasionally engraved
the symbol which disturbs the most,
since grief and mirth
emerge conjoined. The craftsman at his bench
regards it sadly, and a throb
beats in his wrist with blind desire.
He seeks a primordial ornament

addormentato! E tu camminante
procedi piano; ma prima
un ramo aggiungi alla fiamma
del focolare e una pigna
matura alla cesta gettata
nel canto: ne cadono a terra
le provvigioni serbate
pel viaggio finale.

4

Ma dove cercare la tomba
dell'amico fedele e dell'amante;
quella del mendicante e del fanciullo;
dove trovare un asilo
per codesti che accolgono la brace
dell'originale fiammata;
oh da un segnale di pace lieve come un trastullo
l'urna ne sia effigiata!
Lascia la taciturna folla di pietra
per le derelitte lastre
ch'ànno talora inciso
il simbolo che piú turba
poiché il pianto ed il riso
parimenti ne sgorgano, gemelli.
Lo guarda il triste artiere che al lavoro si reca
e già gli batte ai polsi una volontà cieca.
Tra quelle cerca un fregio primordiale

which through the memories evoked
could lead the crude soul on the paths
of mild digressions:
a hint, a sunflower which its yellow petals bares,
and all around, a dance of hares.

che sappia pel ricordo che ne avanza
trarre l'anima rude
per vie di dolci esigli:
un nulla, un girasole che si schiude
ed intorno una danza di conigli . . .

WIND AND BANNERS

The gust that blew the bitter scent
of sea high in the spirals of the vales,
accosted you and rumpled up your hair,
encounter brief against a sky which pales;

the squall that caused your dress to cling,
and modified you to its own imagining—
has returned, detached from you, to find this
place where, from the mount, stones fall to the abyss.

And now that its drunken fury is expended,
the garden finds again the pleasant breeze
which rocked you in the hammock among the trees,
between your wingless flights extended.

Alas, that time will never mold its seeds
in similar design! There is no escaping,
for if there were, our fabled creeds,
would burn with nature in the lightning's strafing.

What does not reproduce, drains away—
and now a group of houses can be seen
distributed along the flanks of a ravine
and decked with banners and with bright display.

The world exists . . . the stuporous heart stands
still, and yields to roving incubi,
the harbingers of evening—unbelieving
in the festivals of famished man's conceiving.

VENTO E BANDIERE

La folata che alzò l'amaro aroma
del mare alle spirali delle valli,
e t'investí, ti scompiglió la chioma,
groviglio breve contro il cielo pallido;

la raffica che t'incollò la veste
e ti modulò rapida a sua imagine,
com'è tornata, te lontana, a queste
pietre che sporge il monte alla voragine;

e come spenta la furia briaca
ritrova ora il giardino il sommesso alito
che ti cullò, riversa sull'amaca,
tra gli alberi, ne' tuoi voli senz'ali.

Ahimé, non mai due volte configura
il tempo in egual modo i grani! E scampo
n'è: ché, se accada, insieme alla natura
la nostra fiaba brucerà in un lampo.

Sgorgo che non s'addoppia,—ed or fa vivo
un gruppo di abitati che distesi
allo sguardo sul fianco d'un declivo
si parano di gale e di palvesi.

Il mondo esiste . . . Uno stupore arresta
il cuore che ai vaganti incubi cede,
messaggeri del vespero: e non crede
che gli uomini affamati hanno una festa.

TWIG HANGING FROM THE WALL

Twig hanging from the wall
as if it were the hand
of a dial to scan the sun's
career and my foreshortened one;
you indicate the dusks,
and thrust root in the plaster
which the day imbues with kindled
lights—and you are bored by the wheel
you spread upon the wall in shade,
you find it infinitely tiresome when
a stale likeness issues
from your hand like smoke,
burdened with its denser
cupola, never dissolved.

But today no longer do you
shade your face, and a veil
which during the night you seized
from an invisible horde is dangling
from your zenith, shining
in the first daylight. Down there
where the sea's face
is uncovered, a three-master laden
with its crew and prey, heels
at a breath—and then slips away.
He who might be watching from above can see
the glistening of the deck and, at the stern,
the water where the rudder leaves no trace.

FUSCELLO TESO DAL MURO

Fuscello teso dal muro
sí come l'indice d'una
meridiana che scande la carriera
del sole e la mia, breve;
in una additi i crepuscoli
e alleghi sul tonaco
che imbeve la luce d'accesi
riflessi—e t'attedia la ruota
che in ombra sul piano dispieghi,
t'è noja infinita la volta
che stacca da te una smarrita
sembianza come di fumo
e grava con l'infittita
sua cupola mai dissolta.

Ma tu non adombri stamane
piú il tuo sostegno ed un velo
che nella notte hai strappato
a un'orda invisibile pende
dalla tua cima e risplende
ai primi raggi. Laggiú,
dove la piana si scopre
del mare, un trealberi carico
di ciurma e di preda reclina
Chi è in alto e s'affaccia s'avvede
il bordo a uno spiro, e via scivola.
che brilla la tolda e il timone
nell'acqua non scava una traccia.

DO NOT TAKE REFUGE . . .

Do not take refuge in the shade
of that dense grove,
like the young hawk which, meteoric,
plunges into the sultry glade.

It is time to abandon the confines
of the cane-brake which seems to sleep,
to penetrate the designs
of a life which disintegrates.

We move in pearly hazes
of vibrant dust,
in a ruthless glare which dazes
and impairs our tired sight.

Still—and you perceive it—rendered flaccid by the play
of arid waves, in this unfavorable hour,
let us not fling our errant lives away
into a bottomless precipice.

Like that cloister of cliffs,
which fades and ravels
in the webs of clouds:
so are our shriveled spirits,

in which illusion burns
with a fire full of ashes—
to dissolve in the clear skies
of one certainty: the light.

NON RIFUGIARTI NELL'OMBRA . .

Non rifugiarti nell'ombra
di quel fólto di verzura
come il falchetto che strapiomba
fulmineo nella caldura.

È ora di lasciare il canneto
stento che pare s'addorma
e di guardare le forme
della vita che si sgretola.

Ci muoviamo in un pulviscolo
madreperlaceo che vibra,
in un barbaglio che invischia
gli occhi e un poco ci sfibra.

Pure, lo senti, nel gioco d'aride onde
che impigra in quest'ora di disagio
non buttiamo già in un gorgo senza fondo
le nostre vite randage.

Come quella chiostra di rupi
che sembra sfilaccicarsi
in ragnatele di nubi;
tali i nostri animi arsi

in cui l'illusione brucia
un fuoco pieno di cenere
si perdono nel sereno
di una certezza: la luce.

THINKING OF YOUR SMILE . . .

to K

Thinking of your smile, it turns into a limpid pool
which by good luck I found among the river's rocks,
a looking glass in which an ivy views her trailing locks
—and over all, the vault of quiet sky.

This I recall, and far would I be from knowing
if your face reveals an artless soul, or if
you might be a wanderer who atones for the world's evil,
wearing his suffering like a talisman.

But this I would tell you: your image evoked
submerges life's griefs like a wave of calm,
and your silhouette converges sharp
upon my memory, like the pinnacle of a young palm.

RIPENSO IL TUO SORRISO . . .

a K.

Ripenso il tuo sorriso, ed è per me un'acqua limpida
scorta per avventura tra le petraie d'un greto,
esiguo specchio in cui guardi un'ellera i suoi corimbi;
e su tutto l'abbraccio d'un bianco cielo quieto.

Codesto è il mio ricordo; non saprei dire, o lontano,
se dal tuo volto s'esprime libera un'anima ingenua,
o vero tu sei dei raminghi che il male del mondo estenua
e recano il loro soffrire con sé come un talismano.

Ma questo posso dirti, che la tua pensata effigie
sommerge i crucci estrosi in un'ondata di calma,
e che il tuo aspetto s'insinua nella mia memoria grigia
schietto come la cima d'una giovinetta palma . . .

I DO NOT ASK OF YOU, MY LIFE . . .

I do not ask of you, my life, fixed
contours, countenances plausible or possessions.
In your unquiet roving, honey and the bark
of wormwood long have left the same impressions.

The heart which every movement loathes
is rarely shaken in diastole,
and sharp is the detonation
of a gun within a silent valley.

MIA VITA, A TE NON CHIEDO . . .

Mia vita, a te non chiedo lineamenti
fissi, volti plausibili o possessi.
Nel tuo giro inquieto ormai lo stesso
sapore han miele e assenzio.

Il cuore che ogni moto tiene a vile
raro è squassato da trasalimenti.
Così suona talvolta nel silenzio
della campagna un colpo di fucile.

OFTTIMES HAVE I MET . . .

Ofttimes have I met the grief of life:
it was the choked source which gurgled,
the shriveling of the scorching leaf upon the stalk;
it was the bludgeoned horse.

Goodness has been to me unknown, aside from
the prodigious which disclosed divine Indifference,
the man of stone amid the somnolence of noon,
the cloud and, high above, the soaring hawk.

SPESSO IL MALE . . .

Spesso il male di vivere ho incontrato:
era il rivo strozzato che gorgoglia,
era l'incartocciarsi della foglia
riarsa, era il cavallo stramazzato.

Bene non seppi, fuori del prodigio
che schiude la divina Indifferenza:
era la statua nella sonnolenza
del meriggio, e la nuvola, e il falco alto levato.

ALL THAT YOU KNEW OF ME . . .

All that you knew of me
was but the whitewash of the wall,
the tunic which invests
our human destiny.

The pall of blue lay far outside
the painting's size;
only a seal of wax denied
the limpid skies.

Or else it was my life's
bizarre mutations,
the glimpses of a glowing clay
which I shall never see.

Thus the integument remained
my true and total substance;
the coals which glowed unquenched
within my soul were ignorance.

If you should come upon a shadow,
shade it is not, for it is I;
and gladly would I offer you
my false ally.

CIÒ CHE DI ME SAPESTE . . .

Ciò che di me sapeste
non fu che la scialbatura,
la tonaca che riveste
la nostra umana ventura.

Ed era forse oltre il telo
l' azzurro tranquillo;
vietava il limpido cielo
solo un sigillo.

O vero c'era il falòtico
mutarsi della mia vita,
lo schiudersi d'un'ignita
zolla che mai vedrò.

Restò cosí questa scorza
la vera mia sostanza;
il fuoco che non si smorza
per me si chiamò: l'ignoranza.

Se un'ombra scorgete, non è
un'ombra—ma quella io sono.
Potessi spiccarla da me,
offrirvela in dono.

I KNOW THE HOUR . . .

I know the hour when the most impassive face
is crossed by a crude and shy grimace,
and fleetingly an unseen pain is manifest.
The travelers in the crowded streets are unimpressed.

You, my words, translate in vain
the secret bite, the wind which blows within the heart.
For he is right who knows the vanity of these:
the song that sobs is the one which can appease.

SO L'ORA . . .

So l'ora in cui la faccia piú impassibile
è traversata da una cruda smorfia:
s'è svelata per poco una pena invisibile.
Ciò non vede la gente nell'affollato corso.

Voi, mie parole, tradite invano il morso
secreto, il vento che nel cuore soffia.
La piú vera ragione è di chi tace.
Il canto che singhiozza è un canto di pace.

GLORY OF THE SUPINE NOON . . .

Glory of the supine noon
when the trees are shadowless, and all
around, exuberance of light turns,
more and more, the midday specters tawny.

The sun, on high, and a desiccated shore.
So my day is not yet past.
Best is the hour beyond the little wall,
which in a plaster twilight holds us fast.

The circling drought; a kingfisher
flutters above a relic of life spent.
The good rain is beyond the squalid firmament,
and yet in waiting is augmented joy.

GLORIA DEL DISTESO MEZZOGIORNO ...

Gloria del disteso mezzogiorno
quand'ombra non rendono gli alberi,
e piú e piú si mostrano d' attorno
per troppa luce, le parvenze, falbe.

Il sole, in alto,—e un secco greto.
Il mio giorno non è dunque passato:
l'ora piú bella è di là dal muretto
che rinchiude in un occaso scialbato.

L'arsura, in giro; un martin pescatore
volteggia s'una reliquia di vita.
La buona pioggia è di là dallo squallore,
ma in attendere è gioia piú compita.

35

HAPPINESS ONCE MADE . . .

Happiness once made,
for you I walk the dagger's blade.
To my eyes you are the flickering half light,
and to my foot, the tight-stretched ice which cracks;
so let him not approach you, who most loves you.

If, coming upon the souls pervaded
by despair, you brighten them, then gentle
is your dawn and only as the nests among the roofs, disturbing.
But nothing curbs the wailing of the boy
whose ball has disappeared among the houses.

FELICITÀ RAGGIUNTA . . .

Felicità raggiunta, si cammina
per te su fil di lama.
Agli occhi sei barlume che vacilla,
al piede, teso ghiaccio che s'incrina;
e dunque non ti tocchi chi più t'ama.

Se giungi sulle anime invase
di tristezza e le schiari, il tuo mattino
è dolce e turbatore come i nidi delle cimase.
Ma nulla paga il pianto del bambino
a cui fugge il pallone tra le case.

THE CANE-BRAKE SPROUTS ITS SPEARS . . .

The cane-brake sprouts its spears
under a sky which no cloud-presage dims;
the thirsty orchard thrusts its shaggy limbs
outside its sheltering frontiers.

Empty, an hour of waiting rises
skyward from the darkening sea.
Upon the water grows a tree
of cloud which, like an ashen tree, capsizes.

The want of you is great, oh absent from this shore
which wastes you in your present or your absent phase.
All slips from its groove, all crumbles;
if you are far, all disappears in haze.

IL CANNETO RISPUNTA I SUOI CIMELLI . . .

Il canneto rispunta i suoi cimelli
nella serenità che non si ragna:
l'orto assetato sporge irti ramelli
oltre i chiusi ripari, all'afa stagna.

Sale un'ora d'attesa in cielo, vacua,
dal mare che s'ingrigia.
Un albero di nuvole sull'acqua
cresce, poi crolla come di cinigia.

Assente, come manchi in questa plaga
che ti presente e senza te consuma:
sei lontana e però tutto divaga
dal suo solco, dirupa, spare in bruma.

PERHAPS SOME MORNING . . .

Perhaps some morning, walking in a vitreous, clear
air, turning I shall see the miracle appear,
the nothingness around my shoulders and the void
behind, and know the terror of the drunken paranoid.

Then suddenly, as on a screen, confusion
of hills, and houses, planted in the usual illusion.
But it will be too late, and I shall be warier
as I move among those men who do not turn, with my
       secret terror.

FORSE UN MATTINO . . .

Forse un mattino andando in un'aria di vetro,
arida, rivolgendomi, vedrò compirsi il miracolo:
il nulla alle mie spalle, il vuoto dietro
di me, con un terrore di ubriaco.

Poi come s'uno schermo, s'accamperanno di gitto
alberi case colli per l'inganno consueto.
Ma sarà troppo tardi; ed io me n'andrò zitto
tra gli uomini che non si voltano, col mio segreto.

VALMORBIA, BLOSSOMING CLOUDS . . .

Valmorbia, blossoming clouds of plants
were traversing your depths on summer breezes;
flowering in us, by happenstance,
oblivion of the world.

The fusillades died down and in the lonely womb
nothing resounded, other than the Leno's heavy boom.
A rocket sprouted on its glowing stem,
releasing burning tears, then dimming them.

The luminous nights were all a dawn
which ushered foxes into my grotto.
Valmorbia, a name—and now, in the bleak memory,
a land from which the night is gone.

VALMORBIA, DISCORREVANO IL TUO FONDO . . .

Valmorbia, discorrevano il tuo fondo
fioriti nuvoli di piante agli àsoli.
Nasceva in noi, volti dal cieco caso,
oblio del mondo.

Tacevano gli spari, nel grembo solitario
non dava suono che il Leno roco.
Sbocciava un razzo su lo stelo, fioco
lacrimava nell'aria.

Le notti chiare erano tutte un'alba
e portavano volpi alla mia grotta.
Valmorbia, un nome—e ora nella scialba
memoria, terra dove non annotta.

YOUR HAND WAS FUMBLING . . .

Your hand was fumbling on the keyboard,
your eyes were scanning on the page
the impossible signs; and every chord
faltered like a soul in bondage.

I saw how everything around was moved
to tenderness to find you helpless and unknowing
in the language most your own; glowing
with pity, out beyond, even the sea was soothed.

Passing the window's azure square, a fleeting
dance of butterflies; a branch was swaying in the sun.
Around us, no single thing could find its parlance,
and mine, or *ours*, became your gentle ignorance.

TENTAVA LA VOSTRA MANO . . .

Tentava la vostra mano la tastiera,
i vostri occhi leggevano sul foglio
gl'impossibili segni; e franto era
ogni accordo come una voce di cordoglio.

Compresi che tutto, intorno, s'inteneriva
in vedervi inceppata inerme ignara
del linguaggio più vostro: ne bruiva
oltre i vetri socchiusi la marina chiara.

Passò nel riquadro azzurro una fugace danza
di farfalle; una fronda si scrollò nel sole.
Nessuna cosa prossima trovava le sue parole,
ed era mia, era nostra, la vostra dolce ignoranza.

THE CIRCLE OF THE CHILDREN . . .

The circle of the children on the shore
was life itself, ringing in the desert;
Among infrequent reeds and brush, in purest
air, the human bush was springing.

The passerby endured the pain
of severance from the antique roots.
In the age of gold, on the shores of the blessed,
a name, or a dress, was held in disdain.

LA FARANDOLA DEI FANCIULLI . .

La farandola dei fanciulli sul greto
era la vita che scoppia dall'arsura.
Cresceva tra rare canne e uno sterpeto
il cespo umano nell'aria pura.

Il passante sentiva come un supplizio
il suo distacco dalle antiche radici.
Nell'età d'oro florida sulle sponde felici
anche un nome, una veste, erano un vizio

FEEBLE SISTRUM ON THE WIND . . .

Feeble sistrum on the wind,
lost cicada,
hardly touched, soon died away
in a darkness once illumined.

The secret spring
trickles from our furthest depths;
our world
stands, wavering.

At a sign from you,
in the fallow air
corrupted vestiges are trembling which the void
will not dissolve anew.

Thus is the gesture checked,
muted the voice;
a stripped life
returns to its source.

DEBOLE SISTRO AL VENTO . . .

Debole sistro al vento
d'una persa cicala,
toccato appena e spento
nel torpore ch'esala.

Dirama dal profondo
in noi la vena
segreta: il nostro mondo
si regge appena.

Se tu l'accenni, all'aria
bigia treman corrotte
le vestigia
che il vuoto non ringhiotte.

Il gesto indi s'annulla,
tace ogni voce,
discende alla sua foce
la vita brulla.

THE WINDLASS SQUEAKS . . .

The windlass squeaks within the ancient well,
the water mounts to the light with which it blends.
In the brimming pail a recollection trembles,
an image smiles within a liquid ring.
I approach that face of evanescent lips:
the past recoils, shatters, and grows old;
it belongs now to another being . . . revolving,
the wheel squeaks again, returning you to the cold
shaft, ah vision, soon removed and now dissolving.

CIGOLA LA CARRUCOLA . . .

Cigola la carrucola del pozzo,
l'acqua sale alla luce e vi si fonde.
Trema un ricordo nel ricolmo secchio,
nel puro cerchio un'immagine ride.
Accosto il volto a evanescenti labbri:
si deforma il passato, si fa vecchio,
appartiene ad un altro . . .
                    Ah che già stride
la ruota, ti ridona all'atro fondo,
visione, una distanza ci divide.

BOARD THE PAPER SHIPS . . .

Board the paper ships lying at anchor
off the singed and blackened shore, and sleep,
little captain, so that you do not hear the rancor
of the malevolent swarms which sail the deep.

Within the orchard walls, the owl darts and plunders,
and coils of smoke are heavy on the roofs.
That instant comes which spoils the thoughtful work
of months: here is the unseen crack, now is the blunder.

The cleft widens, perhaps without the slightest sound.
He who has brought his light to bear, hears his sentence.
It is the hour when only the ship aground
is safe. Moor your fleet within the fence.

ARREMBA SU LA STRINATA PRODA . . .

Arremba su la strinata proda
le navi di cartone, e dormi,
fanciulletto padrone: che non oda
tu i malevoli spiriti che veleggiano a stormi.

Nel chiuso dell'ortino svolacchia il gufo
e i fumacchi dei tetti sono pesi.
L'attimo che rovina l'opera lenta di mesi
giunge: ora incrina segreto, ora divelge in un buffo.

Viene lo spacco; forse senza strepito.
Chi ha edificato sente la sua condanna.
È l'ora che si salva solo la barca in panna.
Amarra la tua flotta tra le siepi.

HOOPOE . . .

Hoopoe, fowl of comedy, slandered
by the poets, you twirl your crest
from the high pole on the chicken coop
and, like a fake weathercock, whirl in the wind;
ambassador of spring, hoopoe, since time
for you stands still and February
will die no more, since everything
outside of you pays homage
to the motions of your head,
and you, madcap, vouchsafe no heed
but turn about, instead.

UPUPA . . .

Upupa, ilare uccello calunniato
dai poeti, che roti la tua cresta
sopra l'aereo stollo del pollaio
e come un finto gallo giri al vento;
nunzio primaverile, upupa, come
per te il tempo s'arresta,
non muore piú il Febbraio,
come tutto di fuori si protende
al muover del tuo capo,
aligero folletto, e tu lo ignori.

LIKE A CYCLONE . . .

Like a cyclone striking
over my bowed head,
a noise of harsh buffoonery.
Once crossed by slanting shadows
from the pines, now the ground is smoking
and the sea below is veiled, less
by trees than by the waves of heat erupting
from the earth's dark veins.
Sometimes more muffled is the boiling up
of waters leashed
beside the long extent of shoal;
then comes the roar of breakers
and the far-flung spray upon the rocks.
As I raise my face, the brays
subside above my head, and shooting
toward the clamor of rough seas
are two white-and-cobalt arrows, two blue jays.

A VORTICE . . .

A vortice s'abbatte
sul mio capo reclinato
un suono d'agri lazzi.
Scotta la terra percorsa
da sghembe ombre di pinastri,
e al mare là in fondo fa velo
piú che i rami, allo sguardo, l'afa che a tratti erompe
dal suolo che si avvena.
Quando piú sordo o meno il ribollio dell'acque
che s'ingorgano
accanto a lunghe secche mi raggiunge:
o è un bombo talvolta ed un ripiovere
di schiume sulle rocce.
Come rialzo il viso, ecco cessare
i ragli sul mio capo; e scoccare
verso le strepeanti acque,
frecciate biancazzurre, due ghiandaie.

SOMETIMES, WALKING . . .

Sometimes, walking down
the stony slopes, eroded
and engorged by autumn rains,
I could not feel
the wheel of seasons turning
in my heart, the trickling
of inexorable time;
but the presentiment of you,
caught from the sudden throbbing
of the air among the boulders
bordering the path—
completely filled my spirit.
Then I came to see,
extended toward some unseen arms,
the rock which sought to free
itself; the hard material divined
the imminent gorge, and trembled;
the tufts of avid reeds swayed,
acquiescent to the occult waters.
Immensity, then you redeemed
even the suffering of the stones:
your exultation justified,
the finite immobility.

SCENDENDO QUALCHE VOLTA . . .

Scendendo qualche volta
gli aridi greppi ormai
divisi dall'umoroso
Autunno che li gonfiava,
non m'era piú in cuore la ruota
delle stagioni e il gocciare
del tempo inesorabile;
ma bene il presentimento
di te m'empiva l'anima,
sorpreso nell'ansimare
dell'aria, prima immota,
sulle rocce che orlavano il cammino.
Or, m'avvisavo, la pietra
voleva strapparsi, protesa
a un invisibile abbraccio;
la dura materia sentiva
il prossimo gorgo, e pulsava;
e i ciuffi delle avide canne
dicevano all'acque nascoste,
scrollando, un assentimento.
Tu vastità riscattavi
anche il patire dei sassi:
pel tuo tripudio era giusta
l'immobilità dei finiti.

Among the scattered rocks, I bowed my head
and to my fancy, salty shapes
appeared: the widespread sea
might be a riddle of rings.
Such is the joy that rapes
the strayed lapwing which escapes
from the closed valley to the shore.

Chinavo tra le petraie,
giungevano buffi salmastri
al cuore; era la tesa
del mare un giuoco di anella.
Con questa gioia precipita
dal chiuso vallotto alla spiaggia
la spersa pavoncella.

I HAVE PAUSED, SOMETIMES . . .

I have paused, sometimes, in grottoes
clinging to your form, vast
or strait, shadowy and bitter.
Seen from their depths, their mouths
marked structures unsurpassed,
stemmed from the skies.
There issued from your resounding
breast ethereal temples,
spires beaming lights:
emerging from each filmy veil,
a crystal city out of the celestial blue,
and its rumbling was no louder than a whisper.
My land was springing from the airy surge,
and from the tumult came the evidence:
returned was the exile to his native innocence.
Thus, father, does one from your exuberance
learn your severe law. And vain
is it to evade: if I attempt it, I am condemned
by even the pitted stone upon my way,
to suffer, nameless as a boulder, or even
as the formless rubble of the plain,
cast by the flooding river from its course,
from life into the tangled forest litter.
In the fate which is forming
there may be a pause,
it holds no further threat.
It is this which the torrent exclaims in its fury,
and the faint breeze echoes.

HO SOSTATO TALVOLTA . . .

Ho sostato talvolta nelle grotte
che t'assecondano, vaste
o anguste, ombrose e amare.
Guardati dal fondo gli sbocchi
segnavano architetture
possenti campite di cielo.
Sorgevano dal tuo petto
rombante aerei templi,
guglie scoccanti luci:
una città di vetro dentro l'azzurro netto
via via si discopriva da ogni caduco velo
e il suo rombo non era che un susurro.
Nasceva dal fiotto la patria sognata.
Dal subbuglio emergeva l'evidenza.
L'esiliato rientrava nel paese incorrotto.
Così, padre, dal tuo disfrenamento
si afferma, chi ti guardi, una legge severa.
Ed è vano sfuggirla: mi condanna
s'io lo tento anche un ciottolo
róso sul mio cammino,
impietrato soffrire senza nome,
o l'informe rottame
che gittò fuor del corso la fiumara
del vivere in un fitto di ramure e di strame.
Nel destino che si prepara
c'è forse per me sosta,
niun'altra mai minaccia.
Questo ripete il flutto in sua furia incomposta,
e questo ridice il filo della bonaccia.

SOMETIMES, ALL OF A SUDDEN . . .

Sometimes, all of a sudden, there comes
an hour when your inhuman heart
can frighten and depart from mine.
Then your music leaves my pitch and key,
your every motion is my enemy.
I turn away, impoverished
of strength; your voice sounds muffled.
I stand a moment on the stony ground
which slopes away toward you, down
to the yellow bluff which, crumbling and furrowed
by the trickling rain,
looms high above your den.
My life is this same arid slope,
a way without an end,
a path wide open to the gathering rivulets—
protracted fragmentation.
It is this plant which,
rooted deep in devastation,
confronts the pounding of the sea
suspended in the wind's erratic forces.
This soil, devoid of vegetation,
has opened up a crack to house a daisy.
In her I sway
before the sea which affronts me,
and miss the silence of my lonely life.
I contemplate the scintillating clay
turned dark by the fairness of the day.
And that which grows in me may be the rancor borne
toward every father by his son, oh sea.

GIUNGE A VOLTE . . .

Giunge a volte, repente,
un'ora che il tuo cuore disumano
ci spaura e dal nostro si divide.
Dalla mia la tua musica sconcorda,
allora, ed è nemico ogni tuo moto.
In me ripiego, vuoto
di forze, la tua voce pare sorda.
M'affisso nel pietrisco
che verso te digrada
fino alla ripa acclive che ti sovrasta,
franosa, gialla, solcata
da strosce d'acqua piovana.
Mia vita è questo secco pendio,
mezzo non fine, strada aperta a sbocchi
di rigagnoli, lento franamento.
È dessa, ancora, questa pianta
che nasce dalla devastazione
e in faccia ha i colpi del mare ed è sospesa
fra erratiche forze di venti.
Questo pezzo di suolo non erbato
s'è spaccato perché nascesse una margherita.
In lei títubo al mare che mi offende,
manca ancora il silenzio nella mia vita.
Guardo la terra che scintilla,
l'aria è tanto serena che s'oscura.
E questa che in me cresce
è forse la rancura
che ogni figliuolo, mare, ha per il padre.

WE NEVER KNOW . . .

We never know what we shall unearth
tomorrow, whether dark or gay;
perhaps our way
to untouched glades will take us
where the waters murmur of eternal youth;
or it may be a long descent
into the last of vales,
in darkness, with the lost memory of the day.
Strange lands may still accord
us welcome: we shall mislay
our recollections of the sun, and falling
out of mind will be the tinkling
of rhymes. Oh the fable which explains our life
will change—how suddenly!—into the dark tale
which is not told! But one thing, still,
you have entrusted, father: that a little
of your gift will always pass in syllables
which we bring with us, bumbling bees.
We shall go far, and always keep
an echo of your voice, as the tarnished grass
recalls the sun, in the darkened courts
among the buildings.
And then, one day, these soundless syllables
that we derived from you
and fed with weariness and silences,
to some fraternal heart will seem
well seasoned with the salt of Greece.

NOI NON SAPPIAMO . . .

Noi non sappiamo quale sortiremo
domani, oscuro o lieto;
forse il nostro cammino
a non tócche radure ci addurrà
dove mormori eterna l'acqua di giovinezza;
o sarà forse un discendere
fino al vallo estremo,
nel buio, perso il ricordo del mattino.
Ancora terre straniere
forse ci accoglieranno: smarriremo
la memoria del sole, dalla mente
ci cadrà il tintinnare delle rime.
Oh la favola onde s'esprime
la nostra vita, repente
si cangerà nella cupa storia che non si racconta!
Pur di una cosa ci affidi,
padre, e questa è: che un poco del tuo dono
sia passato per sempre nelle sillabe
che rechiamo con noi, api ronzanti.
Lontani andremo e serberemo un'eco
della tua voce, come si ricorda
del sole l'erba grigia
nelle corti scurite, tra le case.
E un giorno queste parole senza rumore
che teco educammo nutrite
di stanchezze e di silenzi,
parranno a un fraterno cuore
sapide di sale greco.

IF I AT LEAST COULD PRESS . . .

If I at least could press
into my halting rhythm
some trace of your delirium;
if it were given to me to tune
my stammering parlance to your rigadoon—
I who dreamed of snatching from your lips
the salty words
which art and nature mix,
to sing the melancholy louder
which I, as aging child who never
should have thought, must tolerate.
Instead, I have but threadbare
letters from the dictionaries, and the impure
notes which faithfully vibrate,
creating dreary literature.
I have only those expressions
which, like women advertised,
offer themselves to all demands;
those weary phrases to be soon plagiarized
by tomorrow's student rabble,
to simulate real verse.
And your rumbling voice grows strong:
another azure shadow swells.
My thoughts forsake my heart's designs,
without perception, sense—without confines.

POTESSI ALMENO COSTRINGERE . . .

Potessi almeno costringere
in questo mio ritmo stento
qualche poco del tuo vaneggiamento;
dato mi fosse accordare
alle tue voci il mio balbo parlare:—
io che sognava rapirti
le salmastre parole
in cui natura ed arte si confondono,
per gridar meglio la mia malinconia
di fanciullo invecchiato che non doveva pensare.
Ed invece non ho che le lettere fruste
dei dizionari, e l'oscura
voce che amore detta s'affioca,
si fa lamentosa letteratura.
Non ho che queste parole
che come donne pubblicate
s'offrono a chi le richiede;
non ho che queste frasi stancate
che potranno rubarmi anche domani
gli studenti canaglie in versi veri.
Ed il tuo rombo cresce, e si dilata
azzurra l'ombra nuova.
M'abbandonano a prova i miei pensieri.
Sensi non ho; né senso. Non ho limite.

END OF CHILDHOOD

Roaring, a pulsating ocean, furrowed,
creased and flaked with foam
poured into the cliff-walled cove
and meeting the overflowing mountain stream,
at its torrential outlet, boiled up, yellow.
Colonies of algae, trunks of trees
floated at random on the swell.

Around the hospitable beach
stood only a few houses,
of red weathered brick,
wearing thin wigs of tamarisk
which, hour by hour, turned gray;
wretched creatures, lost in macabre visions.
They were not easy to survey
for one who read in those suspicious
traits the language of a restless soul
who cannot reach decisions.

From every side the hills shut out the view
of sea and dwellings; scattered, the slopes,
with olive trees like pasturing
flocks, or dim as the smoke
of a farm house as it drifts

FINE DELL'INFANZIA

Rombando s'ingolfava
dentro l'arcuata ripa
un mare pulsante, sbarrato da solchi,
cresputo e fioccoso di spume.
Di contro alla foce
d'un torrente che straboccava
il flutto ingialliva.
Giravano al largo i grovigli dell'alighe
e tronchi d'alberi alla deriva.

Nella conca ospitale
della spiaggia
non erano che poche case
di annosi mattoni, scarlatte,
e scarse capellature
di tamerici pallide
piú d'ora in ora; stente creature
perdute in un orrore di visioni.
Non era lieve guardarle
per chi leggeva in quelle
apparenze malfide
la musica dell'anima inquieta
che non si decide.

Pure colline chiudevano d'intorno
marina e case; ulivi le vestivano
qua e là disseminati come greggi,
o tenui come il fumo di un casale
che veleggi

over the blanching face of the sky.
Among stretches of vineyards and of pines,
outcroppings of bald rock were seen,
and the lumpy spines of hillocks:
a passing man, erect
upon a mule against the pure blue,
was etched forever—and in memory.

Seldom did I pass beyond the nearest
mountain tops; nor does
the tired memory dare to vault them.
I know that the roads ran by
ravines, through bramble thickets;
coming out in clearings or by ditches,
and then again, extending
into grottoes damp with molds,
covered with shadow and with silence.
One of these I still recall with wonder,
where every human impulse seems
to sleep, interred
in breezes out of the millennia.
Rarely drops a trickle of air from off the rocks
into that fringe of world which is amazed to breathe.

But one came back from the mountain passes
which settled into an unstable series
of unfamiliar aspects where the rhythm
seemed always imperceptible.

la faccia candente del cielo.
Tra macchie di vigneti e di pinete,
petraie si scorgevano
calve e gibbosi dorsi
di collinette: un uomo
che là passasse ritto s'un muletto
nell'azzurro lavato era stampato
per sempre—e nel ricordo.

Poco s'andava oltre i crinali prossimi
di quei monti; varcarli pur non osa
la memoria stancata.
So che strade correvano su fossi
incassati, tra garbugli di spini;
mettevano a radure, poi tra botri,
e ancora dilungavano
verso recessi madidi di muffe,
d'ombre coperti e di silenzi.
Uno ne penso ancora con meraviglia
dove ogni umano impulso
appare seppellito
in aura millenaria.
Rara diroccia qualche bava d'aria
sino a quell'orlo di mondo che ne strabilia.

Ma dalle vie del monte si tornava.
Riuscivano queste a un'instabile
vicenda d'ignoti aspetti
ma il ritmo che li governa ci sfuggiva.

73

Each moment burned
in the traceless fire of future instants.
To live was an event apart,
hour by hour, and a pounding of the heart.
There was no norm, no groove established,
to divide a joy from sadness.
But reinducted by the country lanes
to the cottage by the sea, asylum
from the childhood shocks and pains,
rapidly I came to yield
outward agreement to every stirring
of the spirit; things clothed themselves in names,
my world took on a center, and a shield.

Such were those virginal days,
in which the clouds were neither monograms nor numbers
but fair-haired sisters whose traveling one shared.
Sprung from other seeds
and watered by another lymph
than ours, were nature's other progeny.
Through her, surcease,
and in her countenance, an ecstasy;
hers the portent which my soul in its confusion
hardly dared to dream of.
Such was my childhood and my illusion.

The years which flew away were short as days;
all certainty was flooded by a sea

74

Ogni attimo bruciava
negl'istanti futuri senza tracce.
Vivere era ventura troppo nuova
ora per ora, e ne batteva il cuore.
Norma non v'era,
solco fisso, confronto,
a sceverare gioia da tristezza.
Ma riaddotti dai viottoli
alla casa sul mare, al chiuso asilo
della nostra stupita fanciullezza,
rapido rispondeva
a ogni moto dell'anima un consenso
esterno, si vestivano di nomi
le cose, il nostro mondo aveva un centro.

Eravamo nell'età verginale
in cui le nubi non sono cifre o sigle
ma le belle sorelle che si guardano viaggiare.
D'altra semenza uscita
d'altra linfa nutrita
che non la nostra, debole, pareva la natura.
In lei l'asilo, in lei
l'estatico affisare; ella il portento
cui non sognava, o a pena, di raggiungere
l'anima nostra confusa.
Eravamo nell'età illusa.

Volarono anni corti come giorni,
sommerse ogni certezza un mare florido

whose power and voracity
soon lent to the quivering tamarisks
their dubious appearance.
The dawn was soon to break in fluent rays
like water on the polished windowsill;
deluded, we ran to open
the creaking garden gate. The artifact
was clear. The clouds weighed heavily
upon an angry sea, which boiled before us.
In the atmosphere hung the suspense
of tempestuous events.
Soon gone, too, were the lands of childhood,
the courtyard explored as if it were a world!
One single turn on the merry-go-round,
and childhood was no more.

Ah, the games among the rushes, of cannibals
with their palm moustaches, the enchanting
harvest of spent cartridge shells!
The golden age was vanishing like the little boats
with bulging sails, on the skyline of the sea.
Certain it is that, waiting for the minute
of violence, I was dumb;
and then, in a conundrum
of calm above the deep-plowed waters,
a wind set in.

e vorace che dava ormai l'aspetto
dubbioso dei tremanti tamarischi.
Un'alba dové sorgere che un rigo
di luce su la soglia
forbita ci annunziava come un'acqua;
e noi certo corremmo
ad aprire la porta
stridula sulla ghiaia del giardino.
L'inganno ci fu palese.
Pesanti nubi sul torbato mare
che ci bolliva in faccia, tosto apparvero.
Era in aria l'attesa
di un procelloso evento.
Strania anch'essa la plaga
dell'infanzia che esplora
un segnato cortile come un mondo!
Giungeva anche per noi l'ora che indaga.
La fanciullezza era morta in un giro a tondo.

Ah il giuoco dei cannibali nel canneto,
i mustacchi di palma, la raccolta
deliziosa dei bossoli sparati!
Volava la bella età come i barchetti sul filo
del mare a vele colme.
Certo guardammo muti nell'attesa
del minuto violento;
poi nella finta calma
sopra l'acque scavate
dové mettersi un vento.

AGAVE* ON THE ROCKS

Sirocco

Oh Sirocco, rabid gale
which burns
the dry, green-yellow hills
and fills the sky with muffled glimmerings;
a puff of clouds, aloft, drifts by
and then is lost.
Perplexing hours, shiverings
of a life which flows away
like water through our fingers;
happenings unapprehended,
lights—shadows, stirrings
of all that is malfirm on earth.
Oh arid wings within the atmosphere,
now I must be the aloe
and adhere
to some crevice of the rock,
and in the sea, must flee the arms of algae
which widen open throats and grip the stones;
and in the ferment of all essences, my buds fast lock
—which know no longer how to open—
and feel my immobility as torment.

Tramontana

And now the anxious rings have disappeared,

L'AGAVE SU LO SCOGLIO

Scirocco

O rabido ventare di scirocco
che l'arsiccio terreno gialloverde
bruci;
e su nel cielo pieno
di smorte luci
trapassa qualche biocco
di nuvola, e si perde.
Ore perplesse, brividi
d'una vita che fugge
come acqua tra le dita;
inafferrati eventi,
luci—ombre, commovimenti
delle cose malferme della terra;
oh alide ali dell'aria
ora son io
l'agave che s'abbarbica al crepaccio
dello scoglio
e sfugge al mare da le braccia d'alghe
che spalanca ampie gole e abbranca rocce;
e nel fermento
d'ogni essenza, coi miei racchiusi bocci
che non sanno piú esplodere oggi sento
la mia immobilità come un tormento.

Tramontana

Ed ora sono spariti i circoli d'ansia

which widened over my heart's lake,
and that vast sputtering of seared
material which slakes the tints, and dies.
Today a will of iron sweeps the skies,
uproots the bushes, racks the palms
and excavates from the compact sea
great furrows edged with slobbering debris.
All shapes are flung about among the outcries.
of the elements; it is a single, mighty clamor
of botched lives: all rises to deflower
the passing hour. Traveling the dome of heaven,
whether leaves or birds—they flutter, and they are no more.
And you who shudder in the thunder
of the winds unquelled,
and clutch to yourself your branches, swelled
with unborn flowers,
how alien you feel those ghosts to be
which swarm the air above the tortured ground,
my subtle life, how fervently
you love your deep-laid roots.

Mistral

Returned is the calm weather: in relief
the waves palaver on the reef.
Along the coast, now quieted, some palm
within its garden hardly sways its head.

che discorrevano il lago del cuore
e quel friggere vasto della materia
che discolora e muore.
Oggi una volontà di ferro spazza l'aria,
divelle gli arbusti, strapazza i palmizi
e nel mare compresso scava
grandi solchi crestati di bava.
Ogni forma si squassa nel subbuglio
degli elementi; è un urlo solo, un muglio
di scerpate esistenze: tutto schianta
l'ora che passa: viaggiano la cupola del cielo
non sai se foglie o uccelli—e non son piú.
E tu che tutta ti scrolli fra i tonfi
dei venti disfrenati
e stringi a te i bracci gonfi
di fiori non ancora nati;
come senti nemici
gli spiriti che la convulsa terra
sorvolano a sciami,
mia vita sottile, e come ami
oggi le tue radici.

Maestrale

S'è rifatta la calma
nell'aria: tra gli scogli parlotta la maretta.
Sulla costa quietata, nei broli, qualche palma
a pena svetta.

81

A breeze caresses the fringes
of the ocean, in an instant's
commotion, a breath which impinges,
and moves again upon its airy way.

Under the shining sky the indolent
billows roll—and then the vast expanse
becomes a looking glass to mirror
in its immense heart my life's predicament.

Look, my tree trunk, you who in this
tardy rapture indicate
each reborn aspect, with the flowering
branches in your hands:

under the dense azure of the sky
a sea bird flies away,
and never rests, for each reflected play
of wing commands him "farther fly."

* A plant, of Mexican origin, frequently seen in the
Mediterranean area. It often grows to a height of six feet
or more and, combined with cacti, forms an effective
windbreak or hedge. The abundant flowers are pale
yellow. The Sirocco is a warm, southerly wind;
the Tramontana is a cold, northerly wind; and the Mistral,
as it is known in Provence, also is northerly.

Una carezza disfiora
la linea del mare e la scompiglia
un attimo, soffio lieve che vi s'infrange e ancora
il cammino ripiglia.

Lameggia nella chiaria
la vasta distesa, s'increspa, indi si spiana beata
e specchia nel suo cuore vasto codesta povera mia
vita turbata.

O mio tronco che additi,
in questa ebrietudine tarda,
ogni rinato aspetto coi germogli fioriti
sulle tue mani, guarda:

sotto l'azzurro fitto
del cielo qualche uccello di mare se ne va;
né sosta mai: perché tutte le immagini portano scritto:
« più in là »!

POOL

Across the tremulous sheet of glass
flitted the mirth of flowering belladonna,
and clouds pressed through the branches of the trees;
rippling and faded, the scene
rose from the depths and surfaced.
A pebble soared and dropped,
breaking the tensed sheen:
the soft mirages shivered and displaced.

But there is more than a design
upon a surface once again serene;
to interrupt is vain:
it strives to live but soon it is effaced;
it drowns if you survey, and sinks again:
it forms and dies, and has not had a name.

VASCA

Passò sul tremulo vetro
un riso di belladonna fiorita,
di tra le rame urgevano le nuvole,
dal fondo ne riassommava
la vista fioccosa e sbiadita.
Alcuno di noi tirò un ciottolo
che ruppe la tesa lucente:
le molli parvenze s'infransero.

Ma ecco, c'è altro che striscia
a fior della spera rifatta liscia:
di erompere non ha virtú,
vuol vivere e non sa come;
se lo guardi si stacca, torna in giú:
è nato e morto, e non ha avuto un nome.

ECLOGUE

To lose oneself within
the undulating gray
of my olive grove was good
in times long past—loquaciousness
of chattering birds
and chanting streams.
How the heels sank in the seams
of the bare ground
among the silver blades
of slender leaves. Dissociated
thoughts came into mind
in the great stillness of the day.

Now vanished are the sky-blue undulations.
The tame pine tree springs
to intercept the vaporous gray;
on high a patch of sky
is burning, a spider's web
is ripped beneath the foot: from all around,
a lost hour is unchained.
Emerging from not far away,
the rumble of a train grows louder.
A shot is crushed upon the vitreous ether.
A flight wings by with the violence of a cloudburst,
an armful of your bitter bark gives out
its last great exhalation, and in an instant
burns and disappears: a pack of hounds explodes
and takes off, raving, on its depredations.

EGLOGA

Perdersi nel bigio ondoso
dei miei ulivi era buono
nel tempo andato—loquaci
di riottanti uccelli
e di cantanti rivi.
Come affondava il tallone
nel suolo screpolato,
tra le lamelle d'argento
dell'esili foglie. Sconnessi
nascevano in mente i pensieri
nell'aria di troppa quiete.

Ora è finito il cerulo marezzo.
Si getta il pino domestico
a romper la grigiura;
brucia una toppa di cielo
in alto, un ragnatelo
si squarcia al passo: si svincola
d'attorno un'ora fallita.
È uscito un rombo di treno,
non lunge, ingrossa. Uno sparo
si schiaccia nell'etra vetrino.
Strepita un volo come un acquazzone,
venta e vanisce bruciata
una bracciata di amara
tua scorza, istante: discosta
esplode furibonda una canea.

The idyll may soon reemerge.
Reformed is the aspect which relies
upon the skies, light palliatives
appear again; the plethora of the snap beans
is blighted and dies back to the roots.
Swift wings are of no avail,
nor the gallant proposition;
nothing abides but the somber cicadas
in the saturnalia of the summer heat;
in the thick, soon come and gone,
a woman's apparition,
quickly dispersed—and it was no Bacchante.
Late to rise was the horned moon.
We were turning back from our
unfruitful wanderings.
Face to face with the world,
no longer could there be discerned
a trace of the frenzy of the afternoon.
Disturbed, we made our way among the briars.
At this hour, in my homeland,
the hares take up their whistling tune.

Tosto potrà rinascere l'idillio.
S'è ricomposta la fase che pende
dal cielo, riescono bende
leggere fuori . . . ;
                    il fitto dei fagiuoli
n'è scancellato e involto.
Non serve più rapid'ale,
né giova proposito baldo;
non durano che le solenni cicale
in questi saturnali del caldo.
Va e viene un istante in un folto
una parvenza di donna.
È disparsa, non era una Baccante.
Sul tardi corneggia la luna.
Ritornavamo dai nostri
vagabondari infruttuosi.
Non si leggeva più in faccia
al mondo la traccia
della frenesia durata
il pomeriggio. Turbati
discendevamo tra i vepri.
Nei miei paesi a quell'ora
cominciano a fischiare le lepri.

CURRENTS

The lads with their bows and arrows
frighten the wrens in their holes.
The lazy azure trickles in the stream
overlaid by indolence,
a pause granted by the stars to those who move
half-dead along the whitened roads.
The tops of the box elders tremble,
high above the hillock ornamented
by an effigy of Summer, mutilated
by the flights of stones;
upon her grows a russet mass of vines,
and all around is a protracted buzz of drones.
But the snub-nosed goddess hardly shows herself,
and everything is bent upon the paper fleet
of vessels drifting slowly downstream.
An arrow flashes in the air,
sticks in a post and tremulously oscillates.
Life is this waste
of banal facts, vain
more than cruel.

FLUSSI

I fanciulli con gli archetti
spaventano gli scriccioli nei buchi.
Cola il pigro sereno nel riale
che l'accidia sorrade,
pausa che gli astri donano ai malvivi
camminatori delle bianche strade.
Alte tremano guglie di sambuchi
e sovrastano al poggio
cui domina una statua dell'Estate
fatta camusa da lapidazioni;
e su lei cresce un roggio
di rampicanti ed un ronzio di fuchi.
Ma la dea mutilata non s'affaccia
e ogni cosa si tende alla flottiglia
di carta che discende lenta il vallo.
Brilla in aria una freccia,
si configge s'un palo, oscilla tremula.
La vita è questo scialo
di triti fatti, vano
piú che crudele.

                    The tribes
of boys with slings return,
whether it be a season or a minute which escapes,
and the dead aspects show themselves unchanged
even though reduced to ashes are all things
and though what hangs from the known tree
is no more its own progeny.
—The lads return . . . ; and thus one day
the circle predetermining our life
presents to us the distant past,
crushed and vivid, printed
on immobile curtains
by an unknown lantern.
And still a dome extends,
sky-blue and blurred
over the thick scum of the pit;
and only the statue is aware
that time is flying, and more and more
it clothes itself in kindled ivy.
And all is carried faster, all descends,
and the eager stream is churning
so that wavelets fracture every mirror:
the little paper ships are wrecked
among the eddies and the soapy ponds.
Good-bye to them!—stones whistle through the fronds;
rapacious fortune is already far away;
an hour sets, its facets blended in one aspect—
and life is cruel more than vain.

Tornano
le tribú dei fanciulli con le fionde
se è scorsa una stagione od un minuto,
e i morti aspetti scoprono immutati
se pur tutto è diruto
e piú dalla sua rama non dipende
il frutto conosciuto.
—Ritornano i fanciulli . . . ; cosí un giorno
il giro che governa
la nostra vita ci addurrà il passato
lontano, franto e vivido, stampato
sopra immobili tende
da un'ignota lanterna.—
E ancora si distende
un dòmo celestino ed appannato
sul fitto bulicame del fossato:
e soltanto la statua
sa che il tempo precipita e s'infrasca
vie piú nell'accesa edera.
E tutto scorre nella gran discesa
e fiotta il fosso impetuoso tal che
s'increspano i suoi specchi:
fanno naufragio i piccoli sciabecchi
nei gorghi dell'acquiccia insaponata.
Addio!—fischiano pietre tra le fronde,
la rapace fortuna è già lontana,
cala un'ora, i suoi volti riconfonde,—
e la vita è crudele piú che vana.

93

CLIFF

A sound of bugles issues
from the precipitous slope
and descends to the shivering sea,
which opens to receive it.
With the shadows, there falls
into the windy throat the word
which earth dissolves in surf;
ablating memory, the world can be reborn.
With the flotilla of the dawn,
the light unfurls its immense sails,
and hope prevails within the heart.
But the daybreak is long gone;
the glimmer has slipped away, and now
condenses over fronds and eminences;
all is closer, more composed,
as if regarded through a needle's eye;
now it is assuredly the end,
and even should the wind be hushed,
still you will hear the file, as it rasps
assiduously the chain which holds us fettered.

CLIVO

Viene un suono di buccine
dal greppo che scoscende,
discende verso il mare
che tremola e si fende per accoglierlo.
Cala nella ventosa gola
con l'ombre la parola
che la terra dissolve sui frangenti;
si dismemora il mondo e può rinascere.
Con le barche dell'alba
spiega la luce le sue grandi vele
e trova stanza in cuore la speranza.
Ma ora lungi è il mattino,
sfugge il chiarore e s'aduna
sovra eminenze e frondi,
e tutto è più raccolto e più vicino
come visto a traverso di una cruna;
ora è certa la fine,
e s'anche il vento tace
senti la lima che sega
assidua la catena che ci lega.

Like a tuneful landslide, the sound is rolling down,
and soon is lost in distance.
With it die away the voices
stored within the arid
convolutions of the sea's crevasses;
the groan of terraces, there
among the vines compressed
by the lacings of their roots.
The cliff has no more room;
hands clutch the limbs of stunted pines;
then the daylight quivers and abates,
a regimen descends, and from the confines
extricates all that only pleads
to last, remains persistently content
to labor infinitely; a mass of rock
slips from the sky and crashes to the shore.

In the faintly falling evening can be heard
a dissolution, and the bugles calling.

Come una musicale frana
divalla il suono, s'allontana.
Con questo si disperdono le accolte
voci dalle volute
aride dei crepacci;
il gemito delle pendìe,
là tra le viti che i lacci
delle radici stringono.
Il clivo non ha più vie,
le mani s'afferrano ai rami
dei pini nani; poi trema
e scema il bagliore del giorno;
e un ordine discende che districa
dai confini
le cose che non chiedono
ormai che di durare, di persistere
contente dell'infinita fatica;
un crollo di pietrame che dal cielo
s'inabissa alle prode . . .

Nella sera distesa appena, s'ode
un ululo di corni, uno sfacelo.

MOIRE*

You bail, and the craft already lists
and the vitreous waters shimmer.
From a grotto we set out into this orange
stretch of seascape, which the breezes disarrange.

We are no longer startled by the call
of bats released by gloomy twilight
in the grotto; and the oar which probed the night,
no longer strikes the rocky wall.

Outside is the sun: it waits
a moment in its course, and fulgurates.
The hollow sky is a refractile
dome of effervescent glass, infrangible.

From his skiff a fisherman throws
his line into the shifting furrows.
He sees the profile of the world condense
upon the bottom, deformed as through a lens.

Abandoned to the rowlocks are the oars,
in the little boat which skirts the shores.
Make sure that you remain immune
to the memory which disturbs this placid noon.

Swarms of flying things surround us, hovering;
the air is a transparent wing.
They vanish: too much light impairs the clarity.
Spent are the thoughts which are too solitary.

MAREZZO

Aggotti, e già la barca si sbilancia
e il cristallo dell'acque si smeriglia.
S'è usciti da una grotta a questa rancia
marina che uno zefiro scompiglia.

Non ci turba, come anzi, nell'oscuro,
lo sciame che il crepuscolo sparpaglia,
dei pipistrelli; e il remo che scandaglia
l'ombra non urta piú il roccioso muro.

Fuori è il sole: s'arresta
nel suo giro e fiammeggia.
Il cavo cielo se ne illustra ed estua.
vetro che non si scheggia.

Un pescatore da un canotto fila
la sua lenza nella corrente.
Guarda il mondo del fondo che si profila
come sformato da una lente.

Nel guscio esiguo che sciaborda,
abbandonati i remi agli scalmi,
fa che ricordo non ti rimorda
che torbi questi meriggi calmi.

Ci chiudono d'attorno sciami e svoli,
è l'aria un'ala morbida.
Dispaiono: la troppa luce intorbida.
Si struggono i pensieri troppo soli.

Soon all will become overcast;
the waves will flower in darker hues.
Now all remains; the blinding shower
of the sun will soon be passed.

Forms and abstracted contours are subverted
by a rippling levitation:
all trenchant powers are diverted
from the path. Life grows by undulation.

It is like a beacon without fire,
prepared to shine throughout the night:
our candle sputters in a greater light
where our commitments and our face ignite.

Let your swollen heart immure
its sorrow in the billow's aperture;
your name is sinking to the ocean's floor
like ballast, to be used no more.

An astral delirium is unleashed in the air,
a calm and shining malady.
Perhaps we shall see the hour which, fair
again, will meet us in an ardent sky.

Threaded with their trailing plants,
the terraced slopes descended
to us below; the ethereal chants
of gleaners in the vineyards blended.

Tutto fra poco si farà piú ruvido,
fiorirà l'onda di piú cupe strisce.
Ora resta cosí, sotto il diluvio
del sole che finisce.

Un ondulamento sovverte
forme confini resi astratti:
ogni forza decisa già diverte
dal cammino. La vita cresce a scatti.

È come un falò senza fuoco
che si preparava per chiari segni:
in questo lume il nostro si fa fioco,
in questa vampa ardono volti e impegni.

Disciogli il cuore gonfio
nell'aprirsi dell'onda;
come una pietra di zavorra affonda
il tuo nome nell'acque con un tonfo!

Un astrale delirio si disfrena,
un male calmo e lucente.
Forse vedremo l'ora che rasserena
venirci incontro sulla spera ardente.

Digradano su noi pendici
di basse vigne, a piane.
Quivi stornellano spigolatrici
con voci disumane.

Oh the summer festival of harvests,
the deviation in the course
of stars!—and everything invests
our somber meditations with remorse.

You speak and do not recognize your voice,
and memory appears to you ablated.
You have passed; to you, your choice
seems free and your life consummated.

What happens now? Once more you feel
your weight, now things compel
the hinges, which were wont to oscillate
—and suspended is the spell.

Ah let us stay here, we are no different!
Motionless, let us remain—who harkens
to a voice already spent?
—submerged in an azure gulf, which darkens.

* "Watered silk," the undulant markings of which
suggest a favorite Montalean motif.

Oh la vendemmia estiva,
la stortura nel corso
delle stelle!—e da queste in noi deriva
uno stupore tinto di rimorso.

Parli e non riconosci i tuoi accenti.
La memoria ti appare dilavata.
Sei passata e pur senti
la tua vita consumata.

Ora, che avviene?, tu riprovi il peso
di te, improvvise gravano
sui cardini le cose che oscillavano,
e l'incanto è sospeso.

Ah qui restiamo, non siamo diversi.
Immobili così. Nessuno ascolta
la nostra voce più. Così sommersi
in un gorgo d'azzurro che s'infolta.

AND HERE THE JOURNEY ENDS . .

And here the journey ends
in the petty occupations which distract
the soul no longer able to lament.
Now equal are the minutes, and immutable
as the windlass of the well.
One turn: one rise of water, one descent.
Another, other water and a squeak of rusty axle.

The journey ends upon this beach
worked over by the slow assiduous tides.
Only indolent trails of smoke are seen
on the waters which soft breezes weave
in coves and, rarely coming into view
in the shining calm among
the islands of the migrant air,
the spine of Corsica or the Capraia.*

You ask if all must disappear
in this residual mist of recollection;
if in this torpid hour or in the breath
of every breaker, all destinies must be fulfilled.
I long to tell you no, that close to you
is the hour which you will pass within a sphere
outside of time; it may be that only the one
who wants to, lives forever: you may be he;
I do not know. I think that for the most of us,
there is no salvation, but who subverts each
plot, eludes each ambush
is he who finds himself. Before I yield,

CASA SUL MARE

Il viaggio finisce qui:
nelle cure meschine che dividono
l'anima che non sa piú dare un grido.
Ora i minuti sono eguali e fissi
come i giri di ruota della pompa.
Un giro: un salir d'acqua che rimbomba.
Un altro, altr'acqua, a tratti un cigolio.

Il viaggio finisce a questa spiaggia
che tentano gli assidui e lenti flussi.
Nulla disvela se non pigri fumi
la marina che tramano di conche
i soffi leni: ed è raro che appaia
nella bonaccia muta
tra l'isole dell'aria migrabonde
la Corsica dorsuta o la Capraia.

Tu chiedi se cosí tutto vanisce
in questa poca nebbia di memorie;
se nell'ora che torpe o nel sospiro
del frangente si compie ogni destino.
Vorrei dirti che no, che ti s'appressa
l'ora che passerai di là dal tempo;
forse solo chi vuole s'infinita,
e questo tu potrai, chissà, non io.
Penso che per i piú non sia salvezza,
ma taluno sovverta ogni disegno,
passi il varco, qual volle si ritrovi.
Vorrei prima di cedere segnarti

I wish to have revealed
to you this path of flight,
labile as the froth or furrow of the sea
in its harrowed reaches.
I give to you, too, my hoarded light
of hope. Tired, I cannot make it bright enough for the new
days. I offer it as hostage
to your fate, that you may escape unscathed.

The journey ends upon these sands,
eroded by the alternating tides.
Deaf to my voice, perhaps your heart
departs already for eternal lands.

* A small island not far from Leghorn.

codesta via di fuga
labile come nei sommossi campi
del mare spuma o ruga.
Ti dono anche l'avara mia speranza.
A' nuovi giorni, stanco, non so crescerla:
l'offro in pegno al tuo fato, che ti scampi.

Il cammino finisce a queste prode
che rode la marea col moto alterno.
Il tuo cuore vicino che non m'ode
salpa già forse per l'eterno.

DELTA

The life curtailed in blind
extravasations I have bound to you:
that one assailed within, who
knows you, suffocated presence.

When time is swelling at its dikes
your fate is turned to its gigantic one;
you crop up, memory, clearer than the dark
regions of your lingering just as now, after the impact
of the rain, the green is denser on the limbs
and on the walls, the cinnabar.

Nothing do I know of you beyond the untold
message which sustains my way:
if you exist as form or fancy, in the cold
mists of a dream, then it is the littoral
which feeds you with its turbid fever
as it thunders with the rising tides.

Nothing of you in the wavering
of the gray hours torn by a blaze
of sulfur, beyond the tugboat's whistle
as she heads for the channel, out of the haze.

DELTA

La vita che si rompe nei travasi
secreti a te ho legata:
quella che si dibatte in sé e par quasi
non ti sappia, presenza soffocata.

Quando il tempo s'ingorga alle sue dighe
la tua vicenda accordi alla sua immensa,
ed affiori, memoria, più palese
dall'oscura regione ove scendevi,
come ora, al dopopioggia, si riaddensa
il verde ai rami, ai muri il cinabrese.

Tutto ignoro di te fuor del messaggio
muto che mi sostenta sulla via:
se forma esisti o ubbia nella fumea
d'un sogno t'alimenta
la riviera che infebbra, torba, e scroscia
incontro alla marea.

Nulla di te nel vacillar dell'ore
bige o squarciate da un vampo di solfo
fuori che il fischio del rimorchiatore
che dalle brume approda al golfo.

ENCOUNTER

Do not, my grief, forsake me
on the street
pelted with hot eddies by the alien
wind, which disappears;
grief dear to the declining breeze
which wafts it to the sea,
where the day breathes out its last antiphonies,
a cloud floats by and, in the sky
flexing, can be seen the cormorant's wing.

The outlet is just beyond the torrent
of sterile waters, alive with stones and lime;
but more is it the outlet of wasted human time,
of faded deeds and lives going down like suns
beyond the puerile
confines which close us in: drab faces,
fleshless hands, horses in rank,
wheels which creak: not lives but vegetations
from the other sea which lies beyond the cloudbank.

We make our way upon a road
of hardened mire, and cannot turn aside,
like people caught in a procession
under a broken vault which crumbles down
almost to the mirroring shop windows
in a viscous breeze which clogs our footsteps
and renders uniform the human gulfweed
stirring behind the rustling bamboo curtains.

INCONTRO

Tu non m'abbandonare mia tristezza
sulla strada
che urta il vento forano
co' suoi vortici caldi, e spare; cara
tristezza al soffio che si estenua: e a questo,
sospinta sulla rada
dove l'ultime voci il giorno esala
viaggia una nebbia, alta si flette un'ala
di cormorano.

La foce è allato del torrente, sterile
d'acque, vivo di pietre e di calcine;
ma piú foce di umani atti consunti,
d'impallidite vite tramontanti
oltre il confine
che a cerchio ci rinchiude: visi emunti,
mani scarne, cavalli in fila, ruote
stridule: vite no: vegetazioni
dell'altro mare che sovrasta il flutto.

Si va sulla carraia di rappresa
mota senza uno scarto,
simili ad incappati di corteo,
sotto la volta infranta ch'è discesa
quasi a specchio delle vetrine,
in un'aura che avvolge i nostri passi
fitta e uguaglia i sargassi
umani fluttuanti alle cortine
dei bambú mormoranti.

Should you too leave me, grief, only
living presage in this cloudy place, like
buzzing spheres would seem
the sound which all around I hear
when an hour is about to strike;
and I am tired from the long waiting
for that soul who knows no dread here on this shore
which the slow swell has overtaken—who does not appear.

Perhaps I still shall catch a glimpse: in the glancing
light, a motion brings me to a puny
sprig, growing in a pot
beside a tavern door.
Reaching out my hand, I sense another life
which becomes mine, remnant
of a form which was removed from me;
not quite are they rings, which twist
about my fingers; they are not leaves but locks.

Then nothing more. Oh submerged one! You disappear
just as you came, and I know nothing of you.
Your life remains your own: already it is lost
among the rare shimmerings of the day. Pray
for me as I descend a path quite other
than a city street
in the dark air, as I accost
the mortal swarms; that I may feel you near;
that I descend with honor and without dismay.

Se mi lasci anche tu, tristezza, solo
presagio vivo in questo nembo, sembra
che attorno mi si effonda
un ronzio qual di sfere quando un'ora
sta per scoccare;
e cado inerte nell'attesa spenta
di chi non sa temere
su questa proda che ha sorpresa l'onda
lenta, che non appare.

Forse riavrò un aspetto: nella luce
radente un moto mi conduce accanto
a una misera fronda che in un vaso
s'alleva s'una porta di osteria.
A lei tendo la mano, e farsi mia
un'altra vita sento, ingombro d'una
forma che mi fu tolta; e quasi anelli
alle dita non foglie mi si attorcono
ma capelli.

Poi piú nulla. Oh sommersa!: tu dispari
qual sei venuta, e nulla so di te.
La tua vita è ancor tua: tra i guizzi rari
dal giorno sparsa già. Prega per me
allora ch'io discenda altro cammino
che una via di città,
nell'aria persa, innanzi al brulichio
dei vivi; ch'io ti senta accanto: ch'io
scenda senza viltà.

RIVIERAS

Rivieras,
a few blades of swordgrass would be enough,
hanging from a bluff
over the sea's delirium;
or two pale camellias
in the deserted gardens
and a blond eucalyptus plunging
among rustlings and mad flights
into the light:
and there, in an instant,
unseen threads are twined about me,
butterfly in a spiderweb
of the quiverings of olives, the stares of sunflowers.

Today mild bondage, rivieras,
of him who easily could succumb
as if to reenact some antique game,
never forgotten.
I recall the acrid potion that you proffered
to the bewildered adolescent, oh shores:
in the limpid mornings
the crests of hills were fused with sky:
on the sands, the undertow was strong,
the counter-thrust of life,
a fever of the world; and in itself
each thing seemed to consume itself.

Oh tossed and harried there
as cuttlefish bones are harried by the waves,

RIVIERE

Riviere,
bastano pochi stocchi d'erbaspada
penduli da un ciglione
sul delirio del mare;
o due camelie pallide
nei giardini deserti,
e un eucalipto biondo che si tuffi
tra sfrusci e pazzi voli
nella luce;
ed ecco che in un attimo
invisibili fili a me si asserpano,
farfalla in una ragna
di fremiti d'olivi, di sguardi di girasoli.

Dolce cattività, oggi, riviere
di chi s'arrende per poco
come a rivivere un antico giuoco
non mai dimenticato.
Rammento l'acre filtro che porgeste
allo smarrito adolescente, o rive:
nelle chiare mattine si fondevano
dorsi di colli e cielo; sulla rena
dei lidi era un risucchio ampio, un eguale
fremer di vite
una febbre del mondo; ed ogni cosa
in se stessa pareva consumarsi.

Oh allora sballottati
come l'osso di seppia dalle ondate

to vanish atom by atom!
To become a wrinkled tree, a rock
scoured by the sea; to melt
away in sunset color; to vanish, flesh,
and gush a spring entranced with sun,
by sun devoured . . .
                    These, oh rivieras,
were the wishes of the ancient youth
beside a rusted paling
who slowly vanished, smiling.

How much, seashores, these cold lights tell
to those who, anguished, fled from you.
Stretches of water can be seen through nets
of labile branches; brown rocks
in dashing spray; dartings of roving
swallows . . .
                    Ah, once upon a time,
oh lands, I could believe you,
funereal beauties, golden convolutions
framing the agony of all being.
                    Stronger, I return
to you today, perhaps, though my heart
melts in cheerful—and atrocious—memories.
Doleful soul of earlier years
and you, new summoning will,
it would perhaps be time for unison
in some calm port of wisdom.

svanire a poco a poco;
diventare
un albero rugoso od una pietra
levigata dal mare; nei colori
fondersi dei tramonti; sparir carne
per spicciare sorgente ebbra di sole,
dal sole divorata . . .
            Erano questi,
riviere, i voti del fanciullo antico
che accanto ad una rósa balaustrata
lentamente moriva sorridendo.

Quanto, marine, queste fredde luci
parlano a chi straziato vi fuggiva.
Lame d'acqua scoprentisi tra varchi
di labili ramure; rocce brune
tra spumeggi; frecciare di rondoni
vagabondi . . .
            Ah, potevo
credervi un giorno o terre,
bellezze funerarie, auree cornici
all'agonia d'ogni essere.
            Oggi torno
a voi più forte, o è inganno, ben che il cuore
par sciogliersi in ricordi lieti—e atroci.
Triste anima passata
e tu volontà nuova che mi chiami,
tempo è forse d'unirvi
in un porto sereno di saggezza.

117

And once more golden voices
will invite with audacious flattery,
oh soul no longer sundered.
Just think: to transform the elegy into a hymn;
to renew oneself, to flag no more.
                    Resembling
these branches, yesterday denuded,
now burgeoning with thrills and juices,
could we but feel
tomorrow in its winds and perfumes
a reflux of dreams, a maddening
urge of voices toward a solution;
and in the sun which clothes you, rivieras,
flower again!

Ed un giorno sarà ancora l'invito
di voci d'oro, di lusinghe audaci,
anima mia non piú divisa. Pensa:
cangiare in inno l'elegia; rifarsi;
non mancar piú.
                        Potere
simili a questi rami
ieri scarniti e nudi ed oggi pieni
di fremiti e di linfe,
sentire
noi pur domani tra i profumi e i venti
un riaffluir di sogni, un urger folle
di voci verso un esito; e nel sole
che v'investe, riviere,
rifiorire!

OCCASIONS

THE BALCONY*

Child's play it seemed
to transmute into the null
that void which had opened before me,
into an uncertain tedium your certain fire.

Now to that vacuum I have added
my every latent motive;
blunted on the hard void is the desire
to serve you, alive.

The life which glimmers dimly
is for your eyes alone to know,
and toward that twilight you lean out
from my unlighted window.

* This belongs to the Motets. Withdrawn from the body
of the text, as a dedication. (Author's note.)

IL BALCONE

Pareva facile giuoco
mutare in nulla lo spazio
che m'era aperto, iu un tedio
malcerto il certo tuo fuoco.

Ora a quel vuoto ho congiunto
ogni mio tardo motivo,
sull'arduo nulla si spunta
l'ansia di attenderti vivo.

La vita che dà barlumi
è quella che sola tu scorgi.
A lei ti sporgi da questa
finestra che non s'illumina.

OLD VERSES

I remember the moth which had entered by the open
window, out of the dusky evening
on that quiet coast scoured by the furious
pounding of the sea spray.
All the twilight air was stirring in the feeble
flickering of that trace which separates the earth
from water; and the beacon, cerulean atonal
point above the Tino rock,
sent out its triple flash
and then subsided in another gold.

My mother was beside me, seated
at the table cluttered with cards erected
two by two like miniature tents
for the lead soldiers of grandchildren
already disbanded and tucked in bed.
From far aloft a mass of wintry air
formed and fell abruptly, and then it poured
over the rugged summit of Corniglia.
Then the darkness was unbroken, and a deep rumbling
came from the sea, insistent as a long
concerto, and the waxing of a pale
and undulating light beyond the hedgerow
crowned by the mountain laurel. Into the brief
space of my room, where the lamplight
quivered in a fuchsia web,

VECCHI VERSI

Ricordo la farfalla ch'era entrata
dai vetri schiusi nella sera fumida
su la costa raccolta, dilavata
dal trascorrere iroso delle spume.
Muoveva tutta l'aria del crepuscolo a un fioco
occiduo palpebrare della traccia
che divide acqua e terra; ed il punto atono
del faro che baluginava sulla
roccia del Tino, cerula, tre volte
si dilatò e si spense in un altro oro.

Mia madre stava accanto a me seduta
presso il tavolo ingombro dalle carte
da giuoco alzate a due per volta come
attendamenti nani pei soldati
dei nipoti sbandati già dal sonno.
Si schiodava dall'alto impetuoso
un nembo d'aria diaccia, diluviava
sul nido di Corniglia rugginoso.
Poi fu l'oscurità piena, e dal mare
un rombo basso e assiduo come un lungo
regolato concerto, ed il gonfiare
d'un pallore ondulante oltre la siepe
cimata dei potòsfori. Nel breve
vano della mia stanza, ove la lampada
tremava dentro una ragnata fucsia,
penetrò la farfalla, al paralume
giunse e le conterie che l'avvolgevano
segnando i muri di riflessi ombrati

the moth flew in and reached the lampshade,
and the fringe of glass beads tinkled, casting
on the wall a pendant band of filaments.

It was a dreadful bug with sharp
proboscis, its eyes encircled, as it were,
with a reddish halo behind which was
the cranium of a human; and if some
hand reached out, it gave a terrifying
hiss which turned us cold with fear.

It thumped again upon the table
and on the panes now closed tight by the wind
and, finding its way once more,
it disappeared in shadow. From the port
of Vernazza the lights blinked
as unseen waves grew higher
in the depths of the night.

And then the moth returned
to the canopy of light, dropped
to the journals on the table and with mad
flutterings, leveled the cards—
                    and that was the end
of all the things that close in a secure
ring like a day, and memory
augments them within, the only
living things in a life which went below ground:
together with the familiar faces, now

eguali come fregi si sconvolsero
e sullo scialbo corse alle pareti
un fascio semovente di fili esili.

Era un insetto orribile dal becco
aguzzo, gli occhi avvolti come d'una
rossastra fotosfera, al dosso il teschio
umano; e attorno dava se una mano
tentava di ghermirlo un acre sibilo
che agghiacciava.

Batté piú volte sordo sulla tavola,
sui vetri ribatté chiusi dal vento,
e da sé ritrovò la via dell'aria,
si perse nelle tenebre. Dal porto
di Vernazza le luci erano a tratti
scancellate dal crescere dell'onde
invisibili al fondo della notte.

Poi tornò la farfalla dentro il nicchio
che chiudeva la lampada, discese
sui giornali del tavolo, scrollò
pazza aliando le carte—
                    e fu per sempre
con le cose che chiudono in un giro
sicuro come il giorno, e la memoria
in sé le cresce, sole vive d'una
vita che disparí sotterra: insieme
coi volti familiari che oggi sperde

no longer lost in sleep but in another shroud;
beside the ancient walls, the beaches,
the tartan loading
pinelogs by the shore each month,
the marks of the torrent still descending
to the sea, its pathway still eroding.

non piú il sonno ma un'altra noia; accanto
ai muri antichi, ai lidi, alla tartana
che imbarcava
tronchi di pino a riva ad ogni mese,
al segno del torrente che discende
ancora al mare e la sua via si scava.

BUFFALO*

A mild inferno fitfully condensed
the surging particolored crowds
in the curving stands loud with megaphones.
Autobuses discharged their loads
in spurts, into the evening. The livid
heat sent off a smoky steam over the
swarming gulf; farther down, an arc
light simulated a stream and the
mob was about to cross. A Negro
dozed in the path of a beam
which cut a swath in the dark; from one
of the boxes several soft, cheerful
women waited for the barge to dock.
I whispered "Buffalo"—and the name worked.
                    I was lost
at once in that limbo where
the voices of blood are deafening and the
prospect is alight with flickers like the flashes
thrown off by a mirror.
I heard the bitter crashes, and all around
I saw the bent and light-streaked backs,
milling about upon the tracks.

* The name of a stadium for cycle races, in Paris. The
occasion is a long-distance race. (Author's note.)

130

BUFFALO

Un dolce inferno a raffiche addensava
nell'ansa risonante di megafoni
turbe d'ogni colore. Si vuotavano
a fiotti nella sera gli autocarri.
Vaporava fumosa una calura
sul golfo brulicante; in basso un arco
lucido figurava una corrente
e la folla era pronta al varco. Un negro
sonnecchiava in un fascio luminoso
che tagliava la tenebra; da un palco
attendevano donne ilari e molli
l'approdo d'una zattera. Mi dissi:
Buffalo!—e il nome agí.
                        Precipitavo
nel limbo dove assordano le voci
del sangue e i guizzi incendiano la vista
come lampi di specchi.
Udii gli schianti secchi, vidi attorno
curve schiene striate mulinanti
nella pista.

KEEPSAKE*

Fanfan comes out the winner; Molly
is sold at auction; a reflector sputters.
With long strides, Surcouf covers the quarterdeck,
and Gaspard, in his hole, counts money.
Snow having fallen in the limpid afternoon,
Cicala returns to his nest.
Fatinitza agonizes in a lapse
of memory, of Tony there remains a shout.
Fake Spaniards gamble at the convent
of the Brigands; but from a pocket
the shrill alarm goes off.
The Marchese del Grillo gets thrown out
into the street again; the unhappy Zeffirino
becomes a clerk once more; the Pharmacist
gets up, and the matches pop on the floor.
The Musketeers leave the convent,
Van Schlisch leaps into the saddle, Takimini
fans himself, the Doll is wound up.
(Imàry goes back to his apartment.)
Larivaudière, magnetic, and Pitou
are stretched out, helter-skelter. Man Friday dreams
of his verdant isle, and dances no more.

* Reduced to purely nominal existence, characters are
recalled here from the following operettas: Fanfan la
Tulipe, La Geisha, Surcouf, Le Campane di Corneville, La
Cicala e la Formica, Fatinitza, La Mascotte, I Briganti,
Il Marchese del Grillo, Primavera scapigliata, Il
Campanello dello speziale, I Moschettieri al Convento,
La Principessa dei dollari, La Figlia di Madama Angot,
Robinson Crusoe. (Author's note.)

KEEPSAKE

Fanfan ritorna vincitore; Molly
si vende all'asta: frigge un riflettore.
Surcouf percorre a grandi passi il cassero,
Gaspard conta denari nel suo buco.
Nel pomeriggio limpido è discesa
la neve, la Cicala torna al nido.
Fatinitza agonizza in una piega
di memoria, di Tonio resta un grido.
Falsi spagnoli giocano al convento
i Briganti; ma squilla in una tasca
la sveglia spaventosa.
Il Marchese del Grillo è rispedito
nella strada; infelice Zeffirino
torna commesso; s'alza lo Speziale
e i fulminanti sparano sull'impiantito.
I Moschettieri lasciano il convento,
Van Schlisch corre in arcioni, Takimíni
si sventola, la Bambola è caricata.
(Imàry torna nel suo appartamento.)
Larivaudière, magnetico, Pitou,
giacciono di traverso. Venerdí
sogna l'isole verdi e non danza piú.

ANOTHER MOON EFFECT

The texture of the carob silhouetted
nude against the drowsy azure,
the ring of voices and the silver fingers
passing by the door's embrasure,

the feather snared; the tramping
feet upon the vanishing jetty,
—and the felucca luffs, her sails slack,
and comes about on the new tack.

ALTRO EFFETTO DI LUNA

La trama del carrubo che si profila
nuda contro l'azzurro sonnolento,
il suono delle voci, la trafila
delle dita d'argento sulle soglie,

la piuma che s'invischia, un trepestío
sul molo che si scioglie
e la feluca già ripiega il volo
con le vele dimesse come spoglie.

TOWARD VIENNA

The baroque convent
made of foam and biscuit,
shaded an inlet of smooth water
and well-provided tables, scattered
here and there with leaves and ginger.

A swimmer surfaced, dripping
under a cloud of gnats,
who inquired about our journey
and told of his voyages beyond the pale.

Indicating the bridge before us which
you cross (he said) with ten cents' toll,
he waved good-bye, and then submerged,
—he was the stream itself . . .
             Understudy
in his place, a dachshund bounced
with a howl from the nearby shed,

sole fraternal voice in the sultry heat.

VERSO VIENNA

Il convento barocco
di schiuma e di biscotto
adombrava uno scorcio d'acque lente
e tavole imbandite, qua e là sparse
di foglie e zenzero.

Emerse un nuotatore, sgrondò sotto
una nube di moscerini,
chiese del nostro viaggio,
parlò a lungo del suo d'oltre confine.

Additò il ponte in faccia che si passa
(informò) con un soldo di pedaggio.
Salutò con la mano, sprofondò,
fu la corrente stessa . . .
                    Ed al suo posto,
battistrada balzò da una rimessa
un bassotto festoso che latrava,

fraterna unica voce dentro l'afa.

GERTI'S CARNIVAL

If the wheel gets caught in a swarm
of spinning stars and the horse
rears up among the crowd; if there snows
upon your hair, and hands, a prolonged shiver
of flitting iridescence, or if the children
blow the plaintive ocarinas
to greet your coming
and the airy echoes flake off
from the bridge over the river;
if the street grows empty and conducts
you to a world blown into a
tremulous bubble of air and light
where the sun accords its greeting to your grace
—perhaps, then, you have regained
the way suggested for an instant by
the molten lead at midnight when
a peaceful year was finished without guns.

And now you would like to pause here where
a filter sifts the sounds,
deriving from them the gay and acrid
vapors which for you compose the morrow:
now you ask for the land where onagers
gnaw lumps of sugar from your hand,
and stunted trees project miraculous buds
for the peacock's beak.
(Ah, your Carnival tonight will be
still sadder than my own, hedged in
with gifts for the absent: carts

CARNEVALE DI GERTI

Se la ruota s'impiglia nel groviglio
delle stelle filanti ed il cavallo
s'impenna tra la calca, se ti nevica
sui capelli e le mani un lungo brivido
d'iridi trascorrenti o alzano i bimbi
le flebili ocarine che salutano
il tuo viaggio ed i lievi echi si sfaldano
giú dal ponte sul fiume,
se si sfolla la strada e ti conduce
in un mondo soffiato entro una tremula
bolla d'aria e di luce dove il sole
saluta la tua grazia—hai ritrovato
forse la strada che tentò un istante
il piombo fuso a mezzanotte quando
finí l'anno tranquillo senza spari.

Ed ora vuoi sostare dove un filtro
fa spogli i suoni
e ne deriva i sorridenti ed acri
fumi che ti compongono il domani:
ora chiedi il paese dove gli onagri
mordano quadri di zucchero alle tue mani
e i tozzi alberi spuntino germogli
miracolosi al becco dei pavoni.
(Oh il tuo Carnevale sarà piú triste
stanotte anche del mio, chiusa fra i doni
tu per gli assenti: carri dalle tinte

rosolio-colored, marionettes and arquebuses,
rubber balls and Lilliputian pots
and pans: the mail box marked these
for each distant friend, the hour that
Januarius was revealed, and silently
the incantation was fulfilled.
Is it Carnival or does December linger
still? I think that if you slightly
turn the stem of the little watch you
wear upon your wrist, all will
slip back into a broken Babelic prism
of forms and colors . . .)

And Christmas comes, and the Day of the New Year
that empties the barracks, and brings back to you
the dispersed friends, and even this Carnival
will come again, which now eludes us
through walls, already cracking.
Do you ask that time stand still for the country
which surrounds you? The great variegated
wings graze you, the loggias emit their
blonde and slender talking dolls; the shafts of
the watermills revolve steadily over babbling ponds.
Would you delay the silver chimes above
the town, and the hoarse call of the dove?
Would you demand the anxious
mornings of your distant shores?

di rosolio, fantocci ed archibugi,
palle di gomma, arnesi da cucina
lillipuziani: l'urna li segnava
a ognuno dei lontani amici l'ora
che il Gennaio si schiuse e nel silenzio
si compí il sortilegio. È Carnevale
o il Dicembre s'indugia ancora? Penso
che se tu muovi la lancetta al piccolo
orologio che rechi al polso, tutto
arretrerà dentro un disfatto prisma
babelico di forme e di colori . . .)

E il Natale verrà e il giorno dell'Anno
che sfolla le caserme e ti riporta
gli amici spersi, e questo Carnevale
pur esso tornerà che ora ci sfugge
tra i muri che si fendono già. Chiedi
tu di fermare il tempo sul paese
che attorno si dilata? Le grandi ali
screziate ti sfiorano, le logge
sospingono all'aperto esili bambole
bionde, vive, le pale dei mulini
rotano fisse sulle pozze garrule.
Chiedi di trattenere le campane
d'argento sopra il borgo e il suono rauco
delle colombe? Chiedi tu i mattini
trepidi delle tue prode lontane?

How everything becomes strange and difficult,
how all has become impossible, you say.
Your life is here where the carrier wheels
rumble endlessly, and nothing
returns except in these misleadings
of the possible. Turn back
to the dead toys where it is denied
so much as to die, and with the time which
pulsates at your wrist and once more
dedicates you to your life among the
heavy walls that do not open
to the panting human vortex,
return to the road where at your side
I share your sadness (to which the molten
lead, reformed, alluded in your evening, and in mine):
turn back to the springs which do not flower.

Come tutto si fa strano e difficile,
come tutto è impossibile, tu dici.
La tua vita è quaggiú dove rimbombano
le ruote dei carriaggi senza posa
e nulla torna se non forse in questi
disguidi del possibile. Ritorna
là fra i morti balocchi ove è negato
pur morire; e col tempo che ti batte
al polso e all'esistenza ti ridona,
tra le mura pesanti che non s'aprono
al gorgo degli umani affaticato,
torna alla via dove con te intristisco,
quella che additò un piombo raggelato
alle mie, alle tue sere:
torna alle primavere che non fioriscono.

TOWARD CAPUA

. . . its spine broken at the curve, with a leap
the blonde Volturno fell, pouring its
floods over the heath and dispersing them
into crevices. Farther down, the profile
of a coachman moved above the hedgerows,
appearing as if on horses,
in a train of dust and jingling bells.
It stopped a moment; the equipage lurched;
everywhere there fluttered the tiniest
of butterflies. Then a furtive beam
lighted the battered grove of cork trees:
laboriously the coach departed; and you
inside, again and ever again waving
a scarf, the starry banner in your hand!
—and the gluttonous river was lost in sand.

VERSO CAPUA

. . . rotto il colmo sull'ansa, con un salto,
il Volturno calò, giallo, la sua
piena tra gli scopeti, la disperse
nelle crete. Laggiú si profilava
mobile sulle siepi un postiglione,
e apparí su cavalli,
in una scia di polvere e sonagli.
Si arrestò pochi istanti, l'equipaggio
dava scosse, d'attorno volitavano
farfalle minutissime. Un furtivo
raggio incendiò di colpo il sughereto
scotennato, a fatica ripartiva
la vettura: e tu in fondo che agitavi
lungamente una sciarpa, la bandiera
stellata!, e il fiume ingordo s'insabbiava.

IN THE PARK AT CASERTA

Where the cruel swan arches
his neck and smoothes his feathers down,
on the surface of the pool, from the leaves,
resounds a sphere, ten spheres,
from the depths flame ten torches,

and a sun wavers
in the early air, over dark-green
domes and the warped globes
of the monkey puzzle tree

which unfastens stone arms
with ease, clutching unremittingly
at the passerby, and unravels
roots and stamens from
some ultimate point.

The knuckles of the Mothers* become rough
as they fumble for the void.

* For "the Mothers" the reader is referred to Goethe,
Faust, Second Part.

NEL PARCO DI CASERTA

Dove il cigno crudele
si liscia e si contorce,
sul pelo dello stagno, tra il fogliame,
si risveglia una sfera, dieci sfere,
una torcia dal fondo, dieci torce,

—e un sole si bilancia
a stento nella prim'aria,
su domi verdicupi e globi a sghembo
d'araucaria,

che scioglie come liane
braccia di pietra, allaccia
senza tregua chi passa
e ne sfila dal punto piú remoto
radici e stame.

Le nòcche delle Madri s'inaspriscono,
cercano il vuoto.

THE LOCAL TRAIN

It was thus, like the poignant
shudder that passes through
the suburbs and raises
to the flagstaffs of towers
the ashes of the day,
like the rainy breeze that
through the bars
assails and reassails
the swaying willows—
it was thus and it was tumult
in the sullen darkness
broken by rare gaps of blue,
until slowly there appeared
the nymphean Entella
flowing quietly from childhood
skies beyond the future—
then other beaches came; the wind changed,
the washing increased on the lines, men
came out into the open, new nests
disturbed the gutters—
it was thus,
have you an answer?

ACCELERATO

Fu cosí, com'è il brivido
pungente che trascorre
i sobborghi e solleva
alle aste delle torri
la cenere del giorno,
com'è il soffio
piovorno che ripete
tra le sbarre l'assalto
ai salici reclini—
fu cosí e fu tumulto nella dura
oscurità che rompe
qualche foro d'azzurro finché lenta
appaia la ninfale
Entella che sommessa
rifluisce dai cieli dell'infanzia
oltre il futuro—
poi vennero altri liti, mutò il vento,
crebbe il bucato ai fili, uomini ancora
uscirono all'aperto, nuovi nidi
turbarono le gronde—
fu cosí,
rispondi?

149

MOTETS

II

Many years, and a harder one
above the foreign lake burnished by the setting sun.
Then you descend from the mountains
to bring me back St. George and the Dragon.*

If I could imprint them on the flag
which sags and flutters at the lash of the north
wind in the heart . . . And, for you, go forth
into a whirlwind of immortal unison.

III**

Frost on the panes; the invalids
are always kin, and always
set apart; at the card tables,
prolonged soliloquies over the plays.

There was your exile. I think again
of mine and of the morning when,
among the rocky reefs,
I heard the crackle of the ballerina bomb.

And the evening fireworks
lasted long: as if for a festival.

A brutal wing appeared, and grazed your palm
—in vain; your card is not this one.

MOTTETTI

II

Molti anni, e uno piú duro sopra il lago
straniero su cui ardono i tramonti.
Poi scendesti dai monti a riportarmi
San Giorgio e il Drago.

Imprimerli potessi sul palvese
che s'agita alla frusta del grecale
in cuore . . . E per te scendere in un gorgo
di fedeltà, immortale.

III

Brina sui vetri; uniti
sempre e sempre in disparte
gl'infermi; e sopra i tavoli
i lunghi soliloqui sulle carte.

Fu il tuo esilio. Ripenso
anche al mio, alla mattina
quando udii tra gli scogli crepitare
la bomba ballerina.

E durarono a lungo i notturni giuochi
di Bengala: come in una festa.

È scorsa un'ala rude, t'ha sfiorato le mani,
ma invano: la tua carta non è questa.

IX

The emerald lizard, if it darts out
of the straw, under the flail
of scorching drought—

the sail, when it lists
and plunges in the waves' abyss
at the outcropping rock—

the noon cannon, fainter
than your heart, and the clock
which strikes the hour
and from it no sound issues—

. . .

and then? In vain the thunder's glint

transforms you into something rich and strange.
Different was your imprint.

XII

I clear your forehead of the icicles
which formed upon it as you crossed the cloudy
heights; lacerated are your wings
by cyclones, and you wake by painful starts.

152

IX

Il ramarro, se scocca
sotto la grande fersa
dalle stoppie—

la vela, quando fiotta
e s'inabissa al salto
della rocca—

il cannone di mezzodí
piú fioco del tuo cuore
e il cronometro se
scatta senza rumore—

. . .

e poi? Luce di lampo

invano può mutarvi in alcunché
di ricco e strano. Altro era il tuo stampo.

XII

Ti libero la fronte dai ghiaccioli
che raccogliesti traversando l'alte
nebulose; hai le penne lacerate
dai cicloni, ti desti a soprassalti.

Midday: the medlar tree lengthens
its shadow on the ground, in the sky
a chilly sun persists, and the other shades
rounding the corner of the alley are
unaware as yet that you are here.

XIII

The gondola, gliding in a strident
glare of tar and poppies,
the stealthy song† exuding out of coils
of rope, the high gates closed
upon you, laughter of masked figures interposed,
fleeing in broken ranks—

one among a thousand evenings, and mine
is the deeper night. Moving below,
a muffled din arouses me fitfully
and renders me kin to the eel-fisherman,
seated intent, upon the banks.

* St. George is the patron saint of Genoa.
** Life in the sanatarium as opposed to life engaged in the
war. The expression "ballerina bomb" was used by the
Italian infantry during World War I to denote a type of
hand grenade equipped with a linen "skirt."
† "The stealthy song" might even be "the song of
Everywhere," from the second act of Offenbach's Tales
of Hoffmann. (Author's note.)

Mezzodí: allunga nel riquadro il nespolo
l'ombra nera, s'ostina in cielo un sole
freddoloso; e l'altre ombre che scantonano
nel vicolo non sanno che sei qui.

XIII

La gondola che scivola in un forte
bagliore di catrame e di papaveri,
la subdola canzone che s'alzava
da masse di cordame, l'alte porte
rinchiuse su di te e risa di maschere
che fuggivano a frotte—

una sera tra mille e la mia notte
è piú profonda! S'agita laggiú
uno smorto groviglio che m'avviva
a stratti e mi fa eguale a quell'assorto
pescatore d'anguille dalla riva.

LOW TIDE

Evenings of cries, when the swing
rocks in the pergola of long ago,
and a dark vapor slightly
veils the quiet sea.

That time is no more. Swift oblique
flights now vault the wall, the decadence
of all is not curtailed, and even the immense
rock which lifted you above the swell
upon the rugged shore, is indistinguishable.

Coming with the breath of spring,
a mournful undertow of lives
engulfed; and in the evening,
black bindweed—your memory
alone resists and strives.

It sweeps the parapets, the distant tunnel
where the train so slowly enters.
Invisible, a lunar flock arrives
to nibble at the distant hills.

BASSA MAREA

Sere di gridi, quando l'altalena
oscilla nella pergola d'allora
e un oscuro vapore vela appena
la fissità del mare.

Non piú quel tempo. Varcano ora il muro
rapidi voli obliqui, la discesa
di tutto non s'arresta e si confonde
sulla proda scoscesa anche lo scoglio
che ti portò primo sull'onde.

Viene col soffio della primavera
un lugubre risucchio
d'assorbite esistenze; e nella sera,
negro vilucchio, solo il tuo ricordo
s'attorce e si difende.

S'alza sulle spallette, sul tunnel piú lunge
dove il treno lentissimo s'imbuca.
Una mandria lunare sopraggiunge
poi sui colli, invisibile, e li bruca.

STANZAS

I seek in vain the site of stirring
of that blood which stays you, endless
ricochet of rings outside the brief
extent of human reckonings,
which called you into being in a waste
of agonies unknown to you, alive in a decaying
swamp of astral rubble. And now
it is lymph which, unforewarned, must trace
the contours of your hands, beat in your pulse
and bring the flame or pallor to your face.

Even the minute network of your nerves
is reminiscent of these voyages,
and your eyes reveal a consuming
ardor dimmed by a stormy passage of foam
now breaking, now condensed, and from the throbbing
in your temples you can feel it vanish in your being
like a noisy flock of pigeons, in the silence
of a drowsy city square, night-fallen.

In you, unaware, converges an aureole
of quivering strings, of which one stood apart
among the others; plucked by a gleaming wing
in flight, this one it was that shuddered
at the fall of night, and envisioned vagrant phantoms
where others fancied hosts of maidens,
or discovered by your lightning flash

STANZE

Ricerco invano il punto onde si mosse
il sangue che ti nutre, interminato
respingersi di cerchi oltre lo spazio
breve dei giorni umani,
che ti rese presente in uno strazio
d'agonie che non sai, viva in un putre
padule d'astro inabissato; ed ora
è linfa che disegna le tue mani,
ti batte ai polsi inavvertita e il volto
t'infiamma o discolora.

Pur la rete minuta dei tuoi nervi
rammenta un poco questo suo viaggio
e se gli occhi ti scopro li consuma
un fervore coperto da un passaggio
turbinoso di spuma ch'or s'infitta
ora si frange, e tu lo senti ai rombi
delle tempie vanir nella tua vita
come si rompe a volte nel silenzio
d'una piazza assopita
un volo strepitoso di colombi.

In te converge, ignara, una raggéra
di fili; e certo alcuno d'essi apparve
ad altri: e fu chi abbrividí la sera
percosso da una candida ala in fuga,
e fu chi vide vagabonde larve
dove altri scorse fanciullette a sciami,
o scoperse, qual lampo che dirami,

a flaw in the unclouded sky,
a stagger in the levers of the world.

In you I see an ultimate corolla
of lightest ash, fast withering.
Willed or involuntary, thus is
your nature: you activate the signal
and then disappear. Oh the twanging of
the tightened bow, the furrow that the billow
plows and inundates! And now
the last bubble rises in the blue. It may be
that damnation is this feckless, bitter darkness
which descends upon the waiting few.

nel sereno una ruga e l'urto delle
leve del mondo apparse da uno strappo
dell'azzurro l'avvolse, lamentoso.

In te m'appare un'ultima corolla
di cenere leggera che non dura
ma sfioccata precipita. Voluta,
disvoluta è cosí la tua natura.
Tocchi il segno, travàlichi. Oh il ronzío
dell'arco ch'è scoccato, il solco che ara
il flutto e si rinchiude! Ed ora sale
l'ultima bolla in su. La dannazione
è forse questa vaneggiante amara
oscurità che scende su chi resta.

IN THE RAIN

A murmur, and your dwelling fades
as in the haze of memory—
and the palm sheds tears, now that impinging
dissolution detains within the torrid greenhouses
even the nude hopes, the thought which still invades.

*"Por amor de la fiebre"** . . . at your side
a vortex leads me. A curtain
radiates vermilion and a window closes.
Now it moves along the familiar slopes,
white eggshell gliding through the mire,
a hint of life between the lights and shades.

From the court your record shrieks
Adiós muchachos, compañeros de mi vida,
and the mask will still be dear to me
if there remains beyond the whirling pool of fate
the little jog which leads back to your path.

I follow the bright showers and, farther down,
in clouds, the trailing smoke from a ship.
A shining rift appears . . .
                    To reach you I invoke
the daring of the stork when, rising
from the cloudy pinnacle, it wings
its way towards Capetown.

*"Por amor de la fiebre": words of St. Teresa. (Author's
note.)

162

SOTTO LA PIOGGIA

Un murmure; e la tua casa s'appanna
come nella bruma del ricordo—
e lacrima la palma ora che sordo
preme il disfacimento che ritiene
nell'afa delle serre anche le nude
speranze ed il pensiero che rimorde.

« Por amor de la fiebre » . . . mi conduce
un vortice con te. Raggia vermiglia
una tenda, una finestra si rinchiude.
Sulla rampa materna ora cammina,
guscio d'uovo che va tra la fanghiglia,
poca vita tra sbatter d'ombra e luce.

Strideva Adiós muchachos, compañeros
de mi vida, il tuo disco dalla corte:
e m'è cara la maschera se ancora
di là dal mulinello della sorte
mi rimane il sobbalzo che riporta
al tuo sentiero.

Seguo i lucidi strosci e in fondo, a nembi,
il fumo strascicato d'una nave.
Si punteggia uno squarcio . . .
                    Per te intendo
ciò che osa la cicogna quando alzato
il volo dalla cuspide nebbiosa
rémiga verso la Città del Capo.

CAPE OF THE MESCO

In the skies above the pit, scored at dawn
by the straight flight of the partridges,
the smoke from the quarries relented
and slowly drifted up the steep defiles.
From the platform of the piledriver
the ripples gushed and, soundlessly capsizing,
sank away in the froth
which your footsteps circumvented.

I see the path that I, like a restless
dog, trod one day where it skirts
the surf and climbs among the boulders,
and here and there is lost in the sparse
pasturage. And all is the same.
An echo of past showers churns
in the wet sand. Damp is the sunshine
on the laboring limbs of the bent
stone-splitters who are plying their hammers.

Figureheads which rise again from
sunken prows and bring me something
of you. An auger cuts
a heart upon the rock—around about,
a rumbling gathers force. I grope in the smoke
but I discern again: the rare motions
of your hands return and your face
dawns upon the windowsill—
your lacerated infancy comes back to me
from the gunfire of a devastated place.

PUNTA DEL MESCO

Nel cielo della cava rigato
all'alba dal volo dritto delle pernici
il fumo delle mine s'inteneriva,
saliva lento le pendici a piombo.
Dal rostro del palabotto si capovolsero
le ondine trombettiere silenziose
e affondarono rapide tra le spume
che il tuo passo sfiorava.

Vedo il sentiero che percorsi un giorno
come un cane inquieto; lambe il fiotto,
s'inerpica tra i massi e rado strame
a tratti lo scancella. E tutto è uguale.
Nella ghiaia bagnata s'arrovella
un'eco degli scrosci. Umido brilla
il sole sulle membra affaticate
dei curvi spaccapietre che martellano.

Polene che risalgono e mi portano
qualche cosa di te. Un tràpano incide
il cuore sulla roccia—schianta attorno
piú forte un rombo. Brancolo nel fumo,
ma rivedo: ritornano i tuoi rari
gesti e il viso che aggiorna al davanzale,—
mi torna la tua infanzia dilaniata
dagli spari!

COSTA SAN GIORGIO*

A will-o'-the-wisp obscures the road with dust.
The lamplighter coasts down and pedals
fast, his ladder on his shoulder.
Another light responds and, all around,
the darkness flickers, and then falls again.

I know, the circle is not breached
and all things fall or rapidly ascend
among the arches. Thus the long months
have slipped away: to me remains a phosphorescent
frost of insects in the mine pits,
a dim veil covering the moon.
                    Once
the sun shone on the pathways of the prodigious
El Dorado, and it was mourning among your forebears.
Now the Idol is here, barred off. He reaches
out his arms among the hornbeam; darkness
obscures his gaze. Speechless, parched
and defeated, almost lifeless,
the Idol hangs upon the cross.

His somber presence permeates.
Nothing returns; all that is unseen
is transformed in the magic fire.
There is no breathing; nothing weighs
in the balance; no more does Maritornes
unhook for us her lantern from the
architrave of the stable.

COSTA SAN GIORGIO

Un fuoco fatuo impolvera la strada.
Il gasista si cala giú e pedala
rapido con la scala su la spalla.
Risponde un'altra luce e l'ombra attorno
sfarfalla, poi ricade.

Lo so, non s'apre il cerchio
e tutto scende o rapido s'inerpica
tra gli archi. I lunghi mesi
son fuggiti cosí: ci resta un gelo
fosforico d'insetto nei cunicoli
e un velo scialbo sulla luna.
         Un dí
brillava sui cammini del prodigio
El Dorado, e fu lutto fra i tuoi padri.
Ora l'Idolo è qui, sbarrato. Tende
le sue braccia fra i càrpini: l'oscuro
ne scancella lo sguardo. Senza voce,
disfatto dall'arsura, quasi esanime,
l'Idolo è in croce.

La sua presenza si diffonde grave.
Nulla ritorna, tutto non veduto
si riforma nel magico falò.
Non c'è respiro; nulla vale: piú
non distacca per noi dall'architrave
della stalla il suo lume, Maritornes.

All is the same; do not laugh:
I know, the grievous grating at the hinges
of the years from the very first one, morning
a limbo in the witless downfall—
and at the last, the screw of the mute
foe, which always impinges.
                    If a clock strikes
from behind the doors, it carries the muffled sound
of the dead puppet, sliding to the ground.

* Slope rising rather steeply from the south bank of the
Arno. Two persons are strolling there. Maritornes is the
wench from Don Quixote, or a similar one. Note that
"El Dorado" was the golden man before it became the
golden land. As for the "dead puppet," he has by this time
fallen into the hands of men, and has nothing to do with
the "mute foe" at the last. The poem is half-written,
but perhaps a further development might be inconceivable.
(Author's note.)

168

Tutto è uguale; non ridere: lo so,
lo stridere degli anni fin dal primo,
lamentoso, sui cardini, il mattino
un limbo sulla stupida discesa—
e in fondo il torchio del nemico muto
che preme . . .
                    Se una pendola rintocca
dal chiuso porta il tonfo del fantoccio
ch'è abbattuto.

SUMMER

The cruciform shadow of the kestrel as it skims
seems unfamiliar to the young shrubs.
And what does the cloud see? The gushing
spring has many synonyms.

Perhaps in the silver darting of the trout
upstream
it is you, Arethusa, maiden dead,
who comes back to my feet.

Here is the kindled humerus, the nugget
turned over in the sun,
the patch of wild cabbage, the tense thread
of the spider on the bubbling foam—

and something which stands and too much
of what will not pass the needle's eye . . .

It takes too many lives to make a single one.

L'ESTATE

L'ombra crociata del gheppio pare ignota
ai giovinetti arbusti quando rade fugace.
E la nube che vede? Ha tante facce
la polla schiusa.

Forse nel guizzo argenteo della trota
controcorrente
torni anche tu al mio piede fanciulla morta
Aretusa.

Ecco l'òmero acceso, la pepita
travolta al sole,
la cavolaia folle, il filo teso
del ragno su la spuma che ribolle—

e qualcosa che va e tropp'altro che
non passerà la cruna . . .

Occorrono troppe vite per farne una.

CONSONANCES

Now that, down below, a vaporous
illusion vacillates and fades away,
something else among the trees
announces the green woodpecker's roundelay.

The hand which reaches to the underbrush
and pierces the tissue of the heart
with yellow stubble
is that which ripens golden incubi
mirrored in the gushing rills
when the noisy cart from Bassareo
brings the frantic bellowing of rams
back to the dry pastures on the hills.

Will you also come back, shepherdess
without flocks, and sit down on my stone again?
I recognize you; only what you read
between the flights which shift and vary
on the pass, I cannot guess.
I ask it vainly of the plain where a mist hesitates
between the flash and fusillade above sparse roofs,
of the occult fever of the express train
on the smoking littoral.

CORRISPONDENZE

Or che in fondo un miraggio
di vapori vacilla e si disperde,
altro annunzia, tra gli alberi, la squilla
del picchio verde.

La mano che raggiunge il sottobosco
e trapunge la trama
del cuore con le puute dello strame,
è quella che matura incubi d'oro
a specchio delle gore
quando il carro sonoro
di Bassareo riporta folli múgoli
di arieti sulle toppe arse dei colli.

Torni anche tu, pastora senza greggi,
e siedi sul mio sasso?
Ti riconosco; ma non so che leggi
oltre i voli che svariano sul passo.
Lo chiedo invano al piano dove una bruma
ésita tra baleni e spari su sparsi tetti,
alla febbre nascosta dei diretti
nella costa che fuma.

ELEGY OF PICO FARNESE*

The pilgrim women who, encamped, prolonged
their litany throughout the night,
adjust their sendals on their heads,
put out the fires and remount the carts.
Peering through portholes in the doors
are flaccid housecats in the bleak dawn,
and a tawny dog lies down
among the fallen fruit of the wild orange
in the shadowy orchard.
Yesterday, all seemed a macerated pulp,
but now this morning, spongelike stones
return to life, and dark sleep wakens
in the kitchen; from the great hearth
merry sounds are heard.
The psalmody drifts back in lighter convolutions,
wind and distance break its voices,
recombining them.

    "Islands of sanctuary,
    courses of air-borne ships;
    raise the shroud,
    reckon the days
    and the months still allowed."

Streets and stairways mounting in a pyramid
densely carved, spiderwebs of granite interspaced
with darkness animated by the trusting eyes
of swine, archetypes tinted with verdigris;
issuing in snatches from the parasols of pines
the song unfolds, muffled in the indigo
diffusing over gaps and valleys, and on the crumbled walls.

ELEGIA DI PICO FARNESE

Le pellegrine in sosta che hanno durato
tutta la notte la loro litania
s'aggiustano gli zendadi sulla testa,
spengono i fuochi, risalgono sui carri.
Nell'alba triste s'affacciano dai loro
sportelli tagliati negli usci i molli soriani
e un cane lionato s'allunga nell'umido orto
tra i frutti caduti all'ombra del melangolo.
Ieri tutto pareva un macero ma stamane
pietre di spugna ritornano alla vita
e il cupo sonno si desta nella cucina,
dal grande camino giungono lieti rumori.
Torna la salmodia appena in volute piú lievi,
vento e distanza ne rompono le voci, le ricompongono.

«Isole del santuario,
viaggi di vascelli sospesi,
alza il sudario,
numera i giorni e i mesi
che restano per finire».

Strade e scale che salgono a piramide, fitte
d'intagli, ragnateli di sasso dove s'aprono
oscurità animate dagli occhi confidenti
dei maiali, archivolti tinti di verderame,
si svolge a stento il canto dalle ombrelle dei pini,
e indugia affievolito nell'indaco che stilla
su anfratti, tagli, spicchi di muraglie.

175

"Grottoes where gleams
the etched Fish,
who knows what other dreams are lost,
since all of life is not interred
in their green sepulcher."

Oh indolent illusion. Why linger here
among the lures of bearded women, in a dizzy void
which the Picano blacksmith, leaning
over the white heat as he strikes
the anvil, drives away?
A different thing is Love—now flash
among the branches of the trees with all your wrath,
your fringe of wings, frowning messenger!
If you cut through to the persimmon's core
and, in the water, mirror faithfully
your forehead's plumage, if you destroy the old tales
out of the dark, and stand guard over the passage
            of the few
among the hordes of human goats,

            ("necklaces of hazel nuts,
            sugar spun by hand
            on the cleavage of the magic
            mass which carries
            down the prayers,
            words of dripping wax,
            words scattered by
            the shining sunflower's seed")

«Grotte dove scalfito
luccica il Pesce, chi sa
quale altro sogno si perde,
perché non tutta la vita
è in questo sepolcro verde».

Oh la pigra illusione. Perché attardarsi qui
a questo amore di donne barbute, a un vano farnetico
che il ferraio picano quando batte l'incudine
curvo sul calor bianco da sé scaccia? Ben altro
è l'Amore e fra gli alberi balena col tuo cruccio
e la tua frangia d'ali, messaggera accigliata!
Se urgi fino al midollo i diàspori e nell'acque
specchi il piumaggio della tua fronte senza errore
o distruggi le nere cantafavole e vegli
al trapasso dei pochi tra orde d'uomini-capre,

(«collane di nocciuole,
zucchero filato a mano
sullo spacco del masso
miracolato che porta
le preci in basso, parole
di cera che stilla, parole
che il seme del girasole
se brilla disperde»)

your splendor blazes in the open. But more discreetly
as from the frigid propylaea, the childhood theater
for many years deserted, its ceilings of dark glass,
its astrolabes, after long
delays upon the ivied balconies
a sign conducts us to the vacant field
where someone has set up a shooting contest.
And here, if your inaudible aid should come,
the little disk will spin up in the air
and shatter at our shots. The day demands
no more than a key. The weather is mild.
The lightning of your garments melts in
the humor of the eye which with its crystal,
refracts all other hues. Behind us, calm, oblivious
to the transmutation, like a lemur rendered once again
sublime, the lad Anacletus is reloading the guns.

* A village in the province of Frosinone.

il tuo splendore è aperto. Ma piú discreto allora
che dall'androne gelido, il teatro dell'infanzia
da anni abbandonato, dalla soffitta tetra
di vetri e di astrolabi, dopo una lunga attesa
ai balconi dell'edera, un segno ci conduce
alla radura brulla dove per noi qualcuno
tenta una festa di spari. E qui, se appare inudibile
il tuo soccorso, nell'aria prilla il piattello, si rompe
ai nostri colpi! Il giorno non chiede piú di una chiave.
È mite il tempo. Il lampo delle tue vesti è sciolto
entro l'umore dell'occhio che rifrange nel suo
cristallo altri colori. Dietro di noi, calmo, ignaro
del mutamento, da lemure ormai rifatto celeste,
il fanciulletto Anacleto ricarica i fucili.

FURTHER STANZAS

When, at your gesture, the last shreds
of tobacco are extinguished in the glass plate,
slowly rising to the ceiling
are the coils of smoke
at which the bishops and the knights gaze
astounded from their chequered board; and other
rings are following that are still lighter
than those on your fingers.

The mirage which sketches towers
and bridges in the sky has vanished
at the first breeze; the unseen window
opens and the smoke is stirred. Down there
below, another flock is on the move: a horde
of men who do not recognize your incense,
of whose chess board you alone
compose the pattern.

It was my former doubt that even
to you the game might be unknown
which transpires on the squares and now is cloud
outside your doors: not cheaply to be soothed
is mortal madness, if your eye's flash
is weak; it asks for other fires, beyond
the heavy curtains, which the god of chance
foments for you when helpful.

NUOVE STANZE

Poi che gli ultimi fili di tabacco
al tuo gesto si spengono nel piatto
di cristallo, al soffitto lenta sale
la spirale del fumo
che gli alfieri e i cavalli degli scacchi
guardano stupefatti; e nuovi anelli
la seguono, più mobili di quelli
delle tue dita.

La morgana che in cielo liberava
torri e ponti è sparita
al primo soffio; s'apre la finestra
non vista e il fumo s'agita. Là in fondo,
altro stormo si muove: una tregenda
d'uomini che non sa questo tuo incenso,
nella scacchiera di cui puoi tu sola
comporre il senso.

Il mio dubbio d'un tempo era se forse
tu stessa ignori il giuoco che si svolge
sul quadrato e ora è nembo alle tue porte:
follìa di morte non si placa a poco
prezzo, se poco è il lampo del tuo sguardo
ma domanda altri fuochi, oltre le fitte
cortine che per te fomenta il dio
del caso, quando assiste.

Today I know what you desire;
subdued, the Martinella* tolls, terrifying
the ivory figurines with the spectral
light of snows. But wins the prize
of the lonely vigil he who can
oppose, before the burning glass
that blinds the pawns, your eyes of steel.

* Perhaps everyone does not know that the Martinella
is the bell of the Palazzo Vecchio, in Florence. (Author's
note.)

Oggi so ciò che vuoi; batte il suo fioco
tocco la Martinella ed impaura
le sagome d'avorio in una luce
spettrale di nevaio. Ma resiste
e vince il premio della solitaria
veglia chi può con te allo specchio ustorio
che accieca le pedine opporre i tuoi
occhi d'acciaio.

THE RETURN*

Bocca di Magra

Here are the southwesterly and the mist
over the lapping sand dunes
and there, concealed by the uncertain cloud
or tossed by the to-and-fro of the foam,
is Duilio, the boatman who is crossing,
straining at his oars; here is
the terser allspice of the pines spreading
among poplars and young willows,
and the flailing windmills, and the footpath
wandering with the wave into the muddy creek,
the poisonous fungating morula; here, still,
are the dilapidated circular steps
meandering down beyond the verandah
in a frozen polychrome of joists,
there it is, listening to you, our old
staircase, vibrating to your voice when, saraband,
you gaily laughed from out the music box,
or when cold Furies blow infernal serpents
and the last shouts die away
upon the shores; and here is the sun
which finishes its course and drops from sight
within the margins of the song—here is
your dark tarantulan bite: I am prepared.

* Aria, in which the Mozartian "Snakes of Hell" may not
entirely account for the final storm. (Author's note.)

IL RITORNO

Bocca di Magra

Ecco bruma e libeccio sulle dune
sabbiose che lingueggiano
e là celato dall'incerto lembo
o alzato dal va-e-vieni delle spume
il barcaiolo Duilio che traversa
in lotta sui suoi remi; ecco il pimento
dei pini che piú terso
si dilata tra pioppi e saliceti,
e pompe a vento battere le pale
e il viottolo che segue l'onde dentro
la fiumana terrosa
funghire velenoso d'ovuli; ecco
ancora quelle scale
a chiocciola, slabbrate, che s'avvitano
fin oltre la veranda
in un gelo policromo d'ogive,
eccole che t'ascoltano, le nostre vecchie scale,
e vibrano al ronzío
allora che dal cofano tu ridésti leggera
voce di sarabanda
o quando Erinni fredde ventano angui
d'inferno e sulle rive una bufera
di strida s'allontana; ed ecco il sole
che chiude la sua corsa, che s'offusca
ai margini del canto—ecco il tuo morso
oscuro di tarantola: son pronto.

PALIO*

So your flight did not stop,
lost in the spinning of the top
at the margin of the thoroughfare:
the contest which thins out
its spirals, up to this point
in the purple pit where
a tumult of souls salutes
the heraldic Tortoise and the Unicorn.

The hoisting of the pennants does not change
your face; too great a flame devoured
the marks which you had noted; latest
announcements, this scent of resin and impending
storm and, too, that tepid oozing
of torn clouds, late glorious salute
of a fate evading even destiny.
A sound of bronze issues from the tower:
the procession marches on, drums
rolling to the Districts' glory.
                    Strange that you
who view the agitated vastness,
the darkened bricks, the wobbling paper
balloon protruding from the animated
phantasms on the face of the huge
clock, the tumbling arpeggios
of the swarms, and the stupor
which invades the conch shell
of the Campo—in your fingers you retain

PALIO

La tua fuga non s'è dunque perduta
in un giro di trottola
al margine della strada:
la corsa che dirada
le sue spire fin qui,
nella purpurea buca
dove un tumulto d'anime saluta
le insegne di Liocorno e di Tartuca.

Il lancio dei vessilli non ti muta
nel volto; troppa vampa ha consumati
gl'indizi che scorgesti; ultimi annunzi
quest'odore di ragia e di tempesta
imminente quel tiepido stillare
delle nubi strappate,
tardo saluto in gloria di una sorte
che sfugge anche al destino. Dalla torre
cade un suono di bronzo: la sfilata
prosegue fra tamburi che ribattono
a gloria di contrade.
                              È strano: tu
che guardi la sommossa vastità,
i mattoni incupiti, la malcerta
mongolfiera di carta che si spicca
dai fantasmi animati sul quadrante
dell'immenso orologio, l'arpeggiante
volteggio degli sciami e lo stupore
che invade la conchiglia
del Campo, tu ritieni

the imperious seal which I believed
to be mislaid, and the light of the long
past is shed on all the heads
and with its lilies, blanches them.

From over there returns an echo:
"Once upon a time . . . " (recalling
the prayer out of the dark that found
its way, one morning, back to you)

 "not a realm but your fine
 trace of filigree which
 touched our walking feet
 and left no sign.

 Under that glacial vault,
 a stony sleep oppresses,
 the voice from down below
 is silent, unless heard by you.

 The crossed bar fails to scan
 the light for him who wanders, lost;
 death speaks with no voice other
 than the one which squanders life."

but here another voice abhors the captive's
cell, to whom that song is worth
less than the scribblings of the
constellated shafts (Giraffe and Goose),
which in the heavens cross and then
fall back in flames. The bleachers groan

tra le dita il sigillo imperioso
ch'io credevo smarrito
e la luce di prima si diffonde
sulle teste e le sbianca dei suoi gigli.

Torna un'eco di là: 'c'era una volta . . .'
(rammenta la preghiera che dal buio
ti giunse una mattina)

«non un reame, ma l'esile
traccia di filigrana
che senza lasciarvi segno
i nostri passi sfioravano.

Sotto la volta diaccia
grava ora un sonno di sasso,
la voce dalla cantina
nessuno ascolta, o sei te.

La sbarra in croce non scande
la luce per chi s'è smarrito,
la morte non ha altra voce
di quella che spande la vita»,

ma un'altra voce qui fuga l'orrore
del prigione e per lei quel ritornello
non vale il ghirigoro d'aste avvolte
(Oca e Giraffa) che s'incrociano alte
e ricadono in fiamme. Geme il palco

as the tired nags go by, greeted by a single
shout. A flight takes off! Ignore it!
Forget the death which seeks
and finds the total of the empty skies,
forget the hectic stammerings of the damned!
There was the day of the quick, you see it,
motionless it appears in the water of the ruby,
peopled by images. The present vanishes
and the finish line is far out there:
beyond the wilderness of penants, on the carillon
of heaven, unrestrained, beyond the gaze
of man—and it was you who saw it there, before.
So rise, until the pivot of the spinning top is blunt
but the groove remains incised. Then, nothing more.

* *The festival held every summer in Siena, in which the
districts compete for the honors. Horse racing and pigeon
flights are traditional events.*

al passaggio dei brocchi salutati
da un urlo solo. È un volo! E tu dimentica!
Dimentica la morte
toto coelo *raggiunta* e l'ergotante
balbuzie dei dannati! C'era il giorno
dei viventi, lo vedi, e pare immobile
nell'acqua del rubino che si popola
di immagini. Il presente s'allontana
ed il traguardo è là: fuor della selva
dei gonfaloni, su lo scampanío
del cielo irrefrenato, oltre lo sguardo
dell'uomo—e tu lo fissi. Cosí, alzati,
finché spunti la trottola il suo perno
ma il solco resti inciso. Poi, nient'altro.

THE STORM
AND OTHER POEMS

SERENATA INDIANA

Indeed ours is the dissolution of the evenings.
Destined for us the streak which from the sea
mounts to the park and wounds the aloes.

You can lead me by the hand, if you pretend
to think you are beside me, if I am mad
enough to go along with you; and what you grip,

what you declare, seems quite within your power.

. . .

Were it your airy life which locks
me to the thresholds—and to this I could
lend face and figure. But it is not,

it is not thus. The octopus which slips
its inky tentacles between the rocks,
can make use of you. It is to him that you

belong and do not know it. Truly you,
you think yourself to be, but you are he.

SERENATA INDIANA

È pur nostro il disfarsi delle sere.
E per noi è la stria che dal mare
sale al parco e ferisce gli aloè.

Puoi condurmi per mano, se tu fingi
di crederti con me, se ho la follia
di seguirti lontano e ciò che stringi,

ciò che dici, m'appare in tuo potere.

. . .

Fosse tua vita quella che mi tiene
sulle soglie—e potrei prestarti un volto,
vaneggiarti figura. Ma non è,

non è così. Il polipo che insinua
tentacoli d'inchiostro tra gli scogli
può servirsi di te. Tu gli appartieni

e non lo sai. Sei lui, ti credi te.

THE EARRINGS

The soot upon the mirror retains
no shade of flights. (Of yours no trace remains.)
Unopposed, the moving sponge blots out
the helpless glimmerings from the golden ring.
For you I sought your stones, the corals,
the strong seductive realm: I shun
the disincarnate goddess; desires for you I bear
until the time of their consumption in your light.
The dragonflies drone outside, the mad dirge
drones, knowing that two lives can hardly count.
Flaccid medusae of the night emerge,
returning to the setting. Your imprint
from below will come: where to your lobes
bleak upturned hands will fix the coral rings.

GLI ORECCHINI

Non serba ombra di voli il nerofumo
della spera. (E del tuo non è piú traccia.)
È passata la spugna che i barlumi
indifesi dal cerchio d'oro scaccia.
Le tue pietre, i coralli, il forte imperio
che ti rapisce vi cercavo; fuggo
l'iddia che non s'incarna, i desiderî
porto fin che al tuo lampo non si struggono.
Ronzano èlitre fuori, ronza il folle
mortorio e sa che due vite non contano.
Nella cornice tornano le molli
meduse della sera. La tua impronta
verrà di giú: dove ai tuoi lobi squallide
mani, travolte, fermano i coralli.

WINDOW OF FIESOLE

Here where the furtive cricket gnaws
the garments of plant silk
and the scent of camphor hardly draws
away the moths that leave powder in the books,
the fledgling bird is clambering up the elm
in spirals and by the fronds the sun
is caught in shade. Another light
and other flames, which do not fulfill,
my scarlet ivy.

FINESTRA FIESOLANA

Qui dove il grillo insidioso buca
i vestiti di seta vegetale
e l'odor della canfora non fuga
le tarme che sfarinano nei libri,
l'uccellino s'arrampica a spirale
su per l'olmo ed il sole tra le frappe
cupo invischia. Altra luce che non colma,
altre vampe, o mie edere scarlatte.

THE RED LILY*

The red lily if it took root one day
within your heart of twenty years'
(the poles shone among the sanddiggers'
sieves, sleek moles dove
into their burrows in the rushes; turrets,
banners overcame the falling rain,
and the transplanting was happily accomplished,
into a new sun, to you, all unaware):

The red lily, on distant crags
already sacrificed
to the mistletoe that stings your scarf,
your hands, with an incorruptible frost—
flower of the grave which, opening to you
where the solemn shores extend
and the din of time no longer harries . . .
will waken the celestial harp
and render death your friend.

* *The flower of Florence. Also, the title of the novel by
Anatole France.*

IL GIGLIO ROSSO

Il giglio rosso, se un dí
mise radici nel tuo cuor di vent'anni
(brillava la pescaia tra gli stacci
dei renaioli, a tuffo s'inforravano
lucide talpe nelle canne, torri,
gonfaloni vincevano la pioggia,
e il trapianto felice al nuovo sole,
te inconscia si compí);

il giglio rosso già sacrificato
sulle lontane crode
ai vischi che la sciarpa ti tempestano
d'un gelo incorruttibile e le mani,—
fiore di fosso che ti s'aprirà
sugli argini solenni ove il brusío
del tempo piú non affatica . . . : a scuotere
l'arpa celeste, a far la morte amica.

THE FAN

Ut pictura . . . The lips which blurt confusion,
the looks, the signs, the days elapsed—
I try to fix them there as in the circle
of the lens reversed, mute and reduced,
but more alive. It was a carousel
of implements and men retreating in that haze
which Eurus battled, and the throbbing dawn
already colors it with purple
and destroys the mist.
The mother-of-pearl is glowing, the dizzy
gorge still claims its foundering victims;
your plumes, however, whiten at your cheeks
and the day may still be won. Oh rain
of blows when you unfurl your arc, oh lightning
crude, oh crashes on the hordes! (Does death
accrue to him who recognizes you?)

IL VENTAGLIO

Ut pictura ... Le labbra che confondono,
gli sguardi, i segni, i giorni ormai caduti
provo a figgerli là come in un tondo
di cannocchiale arrovesciato, muti
e immoti, ma piú vivi. Era una giostra
d'uomini e ordegni in fuga tra quel fumo
ch'Euro batteva, e già l'alba l'inostra
con un sussulto e rompe quelle brume.
Luce la madreperla, la calanca
vertiginosa inghiotte ancora vittime,
ma le tue piume sulle guance sbiancano
e il giorno è forse salvo. O colpi fitti,
quando ti schiudi, o crudi lampi, o scrosci
sull'orde! (Muore chi ti riconosce?)

PERSONAE SEPARATAE

Like the golden scale which glitters
in the gloomy depths and, liquefying,
flows in the corridor between the carob trees,
by now reduced to skeletons, is it so of us,
separated persons through another's eyes? A slight thing
is the word, a slight thing space, in these raw
new, misty moons; what is wanting
and what wrings my heart and holds me here among the
trees, awaiting you, is a vanished sense
or, if you will, the fire which would engrave
parallel figures and concordant shade
on earth, shafts of a sundial, the saplings
of the glade, and fill to overflowing
even the hollow stumps, the habitat of ants.
Too mutilated is the human grove, too faint
the perennial human voice,
too ominous the rent which ravels
over the snowy peaks of Lunigiana. Your form
went out from here and paused beside the river,
where the eeltraps lie upon the shore,
then vanished in the ambient air—
and in that place there was no surging horror;
the light still found your light,
now darkened, even as that
first day turned to night.

PERSONAE SEPARATAE

Come la scaglia d'oro che si spicca
dal fondo oscuro e liquefatta cola
nel corridoio dei carrubi ormai
ischeletriti, cosí pure noi
persone separate per lo sguardo
d'un altro? È poca cosa la parola,
poca cosa lo spazio in questi crudi
noviluni annebbiati: ciò che manca,
e che ci torce il cuore e qui m'attarda
tra gli alberi, ad attenderti, è un perduto
senso, o il fuoco, se vuoi, che a terra stampi,
figure parallele, ombre concordi,
aste di un sol quadrante i nuovi tronchi
delle radure e colmi anche le cave
ceppaie, nido alle formiche. Troppo
straziato è il bosco umano, troppo sorda
quella voce perenne, troppo ansioso
lo squarcio che si sbiocca sui nevati
gioghi di Lunigiana. La tua forma
passò di qui, si riposò sul riano
tra le nasse atterrate, poi si sciolse
come un sospiro, intorno—e ivi non era
l'orror che fiotta, in te la luce ancora
trovava luce, oggi non piú che al giorno
primo già annotta.

THE ARK

The spring storm has turned inside out
the umbrella of the willow,
the April gale has snared
within the yard that golden fleece
which hides my dead,
my trusted dogs, my old
attendants—from that day on, how many
(when the willow was blond and with my sling
I cut away the locks) have fallen
panting into the trap. Certainly
the storm will reunite them all beneath
that former roof, but farther off, much farther
from this fulgurated ground where
blood and lime are boiling in the imprint
of the human foot. The ladle is smoking
in the kitchen, its circle of reflections
frames the bony faces, the pointed
muzzles, sheltered by the magnolia
in the background, if a breath should
blow her there. With a howl
of loyalty the spring storm shakes
my ark, oh my lost ones.

L'ARCA

La tempesta di primavera ha sconvolto
l'ombrello del salice,
al turbine d'aprile
s'è impigliato nell'orto il vello d'oro
che nasconde i miei morti,
i miei cani fidati, le mie vecchie
serve—quanti da allora
(quando il salce era biondo e io ne stroncavo
le anella con la fionda) son calati,
vivi, nel trabocchetto. La tempesta
certo li riunirà sotto quel tetto
di prima, ma lontano, più lontano
di questa terra folgorata dove
bollono calce e sangue nell'impronta
del piede umano. Fuma il ramaiolo
in cucina, un suo tondo di riflessi
accentra i volti ossuti, i musi aguzzi
e li protegge in fondo la magnolia
se un soffio ve la getta. La tempesta
primaverile scuote d'un latrato
di fedeltà la mia arca, o perduti.

DAY AND NIGHT

Even a feather in the air can sketch
your form, the sunbeam gamboling
in a maze of furniture, as if projected
with a mirror by some child upon a roof.
Wisps of haze around the encircling walls
extend the poplars' spires, and down
below, the cutler's parrot ruffs
his neck. Then the sultry night
in the little square, and the footfalls,
and always this labor of sinking, again
to emerge in the same guise, for centuries
or instants, of incubi which never regain
the radiance of your eyes
in the incandescent den—and still the cries
and the same long wails on the verandah
if suddenly the blow resounds which brings
the red to your throat, and tears apart your wings,
oh dangerous harbinger of dawn;
and the cloisters waken, and the hospitals,
to a lacerating blast of trumpets.

GIORNO E NOTTE

Anche una piuma che vola può disegnare
la tua figura, o il raggio che gioca a rimpiattino
tra i mobili, il rimando dello specchio
di un bambino, dai tetti. Sul giro della mura
strascichi di vapore prolungano le guglie
dei pioppi e giú sul trespolo s'arruffa il pappagallo
dell'arrotino. Poi la notte afosa
sulla piazzola, e i passi, e sempre questra dura
fatica di affondare per risorgere eguali
da secoli, o da istanti, d'incubi che non possono
ritrovare la luce dei tuoi occhi nell'antro
incandescente—e ancora le stesse grida e i lunghi
pianti sulla veranda
se rimbomba improvviso il colpo che t'arrossa
la gola e schianta l'ali, o perigliosa
annunziatrice dell'alba,
e si destano i chiostri e gli ospedali
a un lacerío di trombe . . .

YOUR FLIGHT

If you appear beside the fire (amulets
dangle from your tresses
and adorn you with stars)
two lights are vying for you
at the gulley which emerges
from below a vault of briars.

Your robe is torn, in sparks the trampled
bushes bristle up again and
the human tadpoles' swollen pond
flows over in the furrows of the night.

Oh, do not linger at the filthy
fringes, leave the bonfires burning
all around; the pungent smoke
leave to the survivors!

If you should quench the fire
(ash-blonde are the locks
upon the knitted brow, tender
outcast from abandoned skies)
how will the hand of silks and gems
recover from among the dead
its ever faithful?

IL TUO VOLO

Se appari al fuoco (pendono
sul tuo ciuffo e ti stellano
gli amuleti)
due luci ti contendono
al borro ch'entra sotto
la volta degli spini.

La veste è in brani, i frútici
calpesti rifavillano
e la gonfia peschiera dei girini
umani s'apre ai solchi della notte.

Oh non turbar l'immondo
vivagno, lascia intorno
le cataste brucianti, il fumo forte
sui superstiti!

Se rompi il fuoco (biondo
cinerei i capelli
sulla ruga che tenera
ha abbandonato il cielo)
come potrà la mano delle sete
e delle gemme ritrovar tra i morti
il suo fedele?

FLORENTINE MADRIGALS

September 11, 1943

Seal, Herma, with tapes and wax
the hope which, banished from
your mornings, has proved vain.
Over the wall where one can read, "Death
of Baffo Buco"* they are passing
a hand with whitewash. A vagabond
up there is scattering handbills on a cloudy
courtyard. And the uproar passes on.

August 11, 1944

A Bedlington appears, a little cobalt
ewe, in the quivering of the great piers—
Trinity Bridge—upon the water. If the
masters of yesterday (of everyday?)
are vanishing like bilge rats into the sewers, the strokes
which pound your temples, even on the wards
of paradise, are the gong which once more
calls you back to us, my sister.

* Political graffiti, possibly referring to Stalin

MADRIGALI FIORENTINI

11 settembre 1943

Suggella, Herma, con nastri e ceralacca
la speranza che vana
si svela, appena schiusa ai tuoi mattini.
Sul muro dove si leggeva MORTE
A BAFFO BUCO passano una mano
di biacca. Un vagabondo di lassú
scioglie manifestini sulla corte
annuvolata. E il rombo s'allontana.

11 agosto 1944

Un Bedlington s'affaccia, pecorella
azzurra, al tremolio di quei tronconi
—Trinity Bridge—nell'acqua. Se s'infognano
come topi di chiavica i padroni
d'ieri (di sempre?), i colpi che martellano
le tue tempie fin lí, nella corsia
del paradiso, sono il gong che ancora
ti rivuole fra noi, sorella mia.

FROM A TOWER

I have seen the white-winged sparrow
spring from the lightning rod:
by his disdainful flight I knew him,
and by his flute roulade.

I have seen the gay, long-eared
Piquillo bound from the mausoleum,
and clamber up a humid chute
of steps to reach his home.

In window panes of stained glass
I have seen a land of skeletons pass
through flowers in bifore—and one
lip of blood become more mute.

DA UNA TORRE

Ho visto il merlo acquaiolo
spiccarsi dal parafulmine:
al volo orgoglioso, a un gruppetto
di flauto l'ho conosciuto.

Ho visto il festoso e orecchiuto
Piquillo scattar dalla tomba
e a stratti, da un'umida tromba
di scale, raggiungere il tetto.

Ho visto nei vetri a colori
filtrare un paese di scheletri
da fiori di bifore—e un labbro
di sangue farsi piú muto.

THE BLACK TROUT

Reading

Curves on the evening surface:
diplomates in Economics,
Doctors in Divinity,
the trout sniffs such, and goes his way;
his furunculous enlightenment
stems from your lightest curl, unfurled
in the bath, from a sigh ascending
from the hypogeum of your office.

216

LA TROTA NERA

Reading

Curvi sull'acqua serale
graduati in Economia,
Dottori in Divinità,
la trota annusa e va via,
il suo balenio di carbonchio
è un ricciolo tuo che si sfa
nel bagno, un sospiro che sale
dagli ipogei del tuo ufficio.

WIND AT HALF-MOON

Edinburgh

The great bridge fell short of you.
Threading even the sewers I would have made it
to you, at your command. But
now my strength wanes, with the sun
on the glass panes of the verandah.

The man who was preaching on the Crescent
asked me "Do you know where God is?" I knew
and told him. He shook his head. And vanished
in the whirlwind that grappled men and dwellings
and hoisted them aloft, on boiling pitch.

VENTO SULLA MEZZALUNA

Edimburgo

Il grande ponte non portava a te.
T'avrei raggiunta anche navigando
nelle chiaviche, a un tuo comando. Ma
già le forze, col sole sui cristalli
delle verande, andavano stremandosi.

L'uomo che predicava sul Crescente
mi chiese "Sai dov'è Dio?." Lo sapevo
e glielo dissi. Scosse il capo. Sparve
nel turbine che prese uomini e case
e li sollevò in alto, sulla pece.

UPON THE HIGHEST COLUMN

Mosque of Damascus

Upon that pinnacle will stand
the arbiter Christ,
to speak his word.
In the rubble of the seven shores
crow and robin, thorn and sunflower
will prostrate themselves together.

But in that twilight, it was you
upon the high place: dark, your wings
encrusted, maimed by the Antilebanese
snows; and again your lightning
changed the black crown of the brushwood
into mistletoe, and the Column
spelled the Law for you alone.

SULLA COLONNA PIÙ ALTA

Moschea di Damasco

Dovrà posarsi lassú
il Cristo giustiziere
per dire la sua parola.
Tra il pietrisco dei sette greti, insieme
s'umilieranno corvi e capinere,
ortiche e girasoli.

Ma in quel crepuscolo eri tu sul vertice:
scura, l'ali ingrommate, stronche dai
geli dell'Antilibano; e ancora
il tuo lampo mutava in vischio i neri
diademi degli sterpi, la Colonna
sillabava la Legge per te sola.

WINTER LIGHT

When I descended from Palmyran skies
to frosted propylaea and dwarfed palms,
and a clutching at my throat informed
me that you would seduce me,
when from the heavens of the Acropolis I came
and met with baskets, each kilometer,
of murine octopi and ocean eels
(the saw blade of those teeth
upon the shrinking heart!),
when I left the spire
of dawns dehumanized by the cold museum
of mummies and of scarabs (you felt ill,
sole life) and compared the pumice,
jasper, sand and sun, the mire
and the divine clay—
                    to the spark
which bounded I was new, and
soon reduced to ashes.

LUCE D'INVERNO

Quando scesi dal cielo di Palmira
su palme nane e propilei canditi
e un'unghiata alla gola m'avvertí
che mi avresti rapito,
quando scesi dal cielo dell'Acropoli
e incontrai, a chilometri, cavagni
di polpi e di murene
(la sega di quei denti
sul cuore rattrappito!),
quando lasciai le cime delle aurore
disumane pel gelido museo
di mummie e scarabei (tu stavi male,
unica vita) e confrontai la pomice
e il diaspro, la sabbia e il sole, il fango
e l'argilla divina—
           alla scintilla
che si levò fui nuovo e incenerito.

AS AN "HOMAGE TO RIMBAUD"

Lately broken from the cocoon,
brave butterfly who from the rostrum
would deflower the exile of Charleville—
oh do not follow him in his rapacious
partridge's flight; let fall no broken
feather, no foliage of gardenia
upon the asphalt ice!
More terrible will be your course if risen
on these pollinated wings of silk;
in the scarlet nimbus you envision,
daughter of the sun, yourself as servant
of his budding thought and now
as mistress of his eminence.

PER UN «OMAGGIO A RIMBAUD»

Tardi uscita da bozzolo, mirabile
farfalla che disfiori da una cattedra
l'esule di Charleville,
oh non seguirlo nel suo rapinoso
volo di starna, non lasciar cadere
piume stroncate, foglie di gardenia
sul nero ghiaccio dell'asfalto! Il volo
tuo sarà più terribile se alzato
da quest'ali di polline e di seta
nell'alone scarlatto in cui tu credi,
figlia del sole, serva del suo primo
pensiero e ormai padrona sua lassú . . .

EZEKIEL SAW THE WHEEL

Did you deliver me, stranger's hand,
from the ivy's cool entanglement?
I was leaning over the viscid pool;
the air was black and only a vein
of onyx quivered in the depths,
a strand of wistaria in a gale.
but the hand did not relinquish:
it grew colder in the dark air,
and the rain which broke loose
over my hair (and yours of that time,
too fine, too smooth), searched stubbornly for
traces buried in me by a mound,
by a hill of sand which I had piled
within my heart in order to drown out
your voice, to tread it down in the narrow
ring that transfigures everything—
scraped, brought to light through prints
of slippers on the drying mud, the splinter,
fiber of your cross within the rotting pulp
of broken beams, the smile of the skull
which intervened when the threatening

EZEKIEL SAW THE WHEEL

Ghermito m'hai dall'intrico
dell'edra, mano straniera?
M'ero appoggiato alla vasca
viscida, l'aria era nera,
solo una vena d'onice tremava
nel fondo, quale stelo alla burrasca.
Ma la mano non si distolse,
nel buio si fece piú diaccia
e la pioggia che si disciolse
sui miei capelli, sui tuoi
d'allora, troppo tenui, troppo lisci,
frugava tenace la traccia
in me seppellita da un cumulo,
da un monte di sabbia che avevo
in cuore ammassato per giungere
a soffocar la tua voce,
a spingerla in giú, dentro il breve
cerchio che tutto transforma,
raspava, portava all'aperto
con l'orma delle pianelle
sul fango indurito, la scheggia,
la fibra della tua croce
in polpa marcita di vecchie
putrelle schiantate, il sorriso
di teschio che a noi si frappose

wheel appeared among reflections
of the dawn and when, turned into blood,
the petals of the peachtree dropped upon me
and with them, now as at that time,
thy claw.

quando la Ruota minacciosa apparve
tra riflessi d'aurora, e fatti sangue
i petali del pesco su me scesero
e con essi
il tuo artiglio, come ora.

THE WOODCOCK

Where you are lying after the short shot
(your voice boils up again, red-black,
ragoût of earth and heaven, on a slow fire)
I too will hide and simmer in the ditch.

The sob would plead for mercy. Sweeter
it would have been to live than founder
in this sediment, easier to relinquish to the wind
than to this mire, gristle on the flame.

In my breast I feel your wound, under a
clot of wings: my heavy flight
attempts the wall and of us two,
remains but a feather on the frosty ilex.

Squabbles of homes, loves, nests of
marble eggs divine. Bud,
gem on the perennials, the grub now glimmers
in the gloom; Jove is entombed.

IL GALLO CEDRONE

Dove t'abbatti dopo il breve sparo
(la tua voce ribolle, rossonero
salmì di cielo e terra a lento fuoco)
anch'io riparo, brucio anch'io nel fosso.

Chiede aiuto il singulto. Era più dolce
vivere che affondare in questo magma,
più facile disfarsi al vento che
qui nel limo, incrostati sulla fiamma.

Sento nel petto la tua piaga, sotto
un grumo d'ala; il mio pesante volo
tenta un muro e di noi solo rimane
qualche piuma sull'ilice brinata.

Zuffe di nidi, amori, nidi d'uova
marmorate, divine! Ora la gemma
delle piante perenni, come il bruco,
luccica al buio, Giove è sotterrato.

THE PROCESSIONS OF 1949

Heat flashes at the point of no return,
livid, cloud-invested hour
and then an even worse effulgence:
clamor of wheels and of denouncements
from the foothills,
a retching and the acrid scents of vomitus
infect the sod for us, your faithful,

         . . . were it not
for your escape, in vitro, in the lake,
I would be entering a soap-bubble filled with gnats.

Who lies the most, who whines? Yours has been
the everlasting instant since you first occurred.
Your furiously angelic virtue, with a glove, deterred
the itinerant Cybele and all her Corybants.

LE PROCESSIONI DEL 1949

Lampi d'afa sul punto del distacco,
livida ora annebbiata,
poi un alone anche peggiore, un bombito
di ruote e di querele dalle prime
rampe della collina,
un rigurgito, un tanfo acre che infetta
le zolle a noi devote,

       . . . se non fosse
per quel tuo scarto in vitro, sulla gora,
entro una bolla di sapone e insetti.

Chi mente piú, chi geme? Fu il tuo istante
di sempre, dacché appari.
La tua virtú furiosamente angelica
ha scacciato col guanto i madonnari
pellegrini, Cibele e i Coribanti.

CLOUDS MAGENTA-COLOR

Clouds magenta-color were gathering
in Fingal's cave beyond the coast
when I said, "My angel,
pedal!" and with a leap
the tandem cleared the mire and
took off among the briars of the ridge.

Clouds copper-color formed
a bridge to span the spires,
the seamy moors, of Agliena when
you told me "Stand!"—and then
your ebony wing filled the horizon
with an unsustainable vast shivering.

Like Pafnuzio in the desert, too much
did I, vanquished, yearn to conquer you.
I fly, I stand with you; to die
or live is but a single turn, a tempest
tinted with your color, your breath's heat
within the cavern—soft pedal-point—
and barely quivering.

NUBI COLOR MAGENTA . . .

Nubi color magenta s'addensavano
nella grotta di Fingal d'oltrecosta
quando dissi "pedala,
angelo mio!" e con un salto
il tandem si staccò dal fango, sciolse
il volo tra le bacche del rialto.

Nubi color di rame si piegavano
a ponte sulle spire dell'Agliena,
sulle biancane rugginose quando
ti dissi "resta!," e la tua ala d'ebano
occupò l'orizzonte
col suo fremito lungo, insostenibile.

Come Pafnuzio nel deserto, troppo
volli vincerti, io vinto.
Volo con te, resto con te; morire,
vivere è un punto solo, un groppo tinto
del tuo colore, caldo del respiro
della caverna, fondo, appena udibile.

PER ALBUM

I began before the day
to cast the hook for you.
But in the dark and turbid pools
I saw no flickering tail;
no wind came to hail your mark
out of the Monferrinian hills.
Always on the watch for you
I went on with my day, larva tadpole
feathered feet of the scrambling grouse
gazelle zebus okapi
black cloud, hailstorm
before the vintage; rambling, I gleaned between
the saturated rows and did not find you.
I continued until late,
not knowing that to me alone
—Sand Soda Soap, the dovecote
from which your flight began: the scullery—
three little drawers would open.
You vanished thus into a dim horizon.
No thought exists which could by stealth ensnare the
              lightning
but having perceived the flash one never could forego it.
I stretched myself below your cherry tree—
Too rich was I already to contain your vital wealth.

PER ALBUM

Ho cominciato anzi giorno
a buttar l'amo per te (lo chiamavo "il lamo").
Ma nessun guizzo di coda
scorgevo nei pozzi limosi,
nessun vento veniva col tuo indizio
dai colli monferrini.
Ho continuato il mio giorno
sempre spiando te, larva girino
frangia di rampicante francolino
gazzella zebú ocàpi
nuvola nera grandine
prima della vendemmia, ho spigolato
tra i filari inzuppati senza trovarti.
Ho proseguito fino a tardi
senza sapere che tre cassettine
—SABBIA SODA SAPONE, la piccionaia
da cui partí il tuo volo: da una cucina,—
si sarebbero aperte per me solo.
Cosí sparisti nell'orizzonte incerto.
Non c'è pensiero che imprigioni il fulmine
ma chi ha veduto la luce non se ne priva.
Mi stesi al piede del tuo ciliegio, ero
già troppo ricco per contenerti viva.

FROM A SWISS LAKE

One day I too, my Renard, was
the "murdered poet"; there, in a grotto
formed by the burnt hazel nut grove;
I saw in that charred den your face,
alight with a golden circle
which blazed and waned, at last conforming
to your nimbus, and therein vanishing.
Disquieted and anxious, I invoked
my dissolution in that symbol of your life overt,
bitter, fragile and still overpowering.

Is it you who glimmers in the gloom? I step
into that throbbing furrow upon a red-hot path,
eagerly I, a stranger, still fall
upon the traces of your predatory
hooflet (almost indiscernible,
its starry imprint); and a black duck,
risen from the far confines of the lake, accompanies me
to the new fire, there to be consumed.

DA UN LAGO SVIZZERO

Mia volpe, un giorno fui anch'io il "poeta
assassinato": là nel noccioleto
raso, dove fa grotta, da un falò;
in quella tana un tondo di zecchino
accendeva il tuo viso, poi calava
lento per la sua via fino a toccare
un nimbo, ove stemprarsi; ed io ansioso
invocavo la fine su quel fondo
segno della tua vita aperta, amara,
atrocemente fragile e pur forte.

Sei tu che brilli al buio? Entro quel solco
pulsante, in una pista arroventata,
àlacre sulla traccia del tuo lieve
zampetto di predace (un'orma quasi
invisibile, a stella) io, straniero,
ancora piombo; e a volo alzata un'anitra
nera, dal fondolago, fino al nuovo
incendio mi fa strada, per bruciarsi.

ANNIVERSARY

Since the time of your birth,
my Renard, I have been kneeling
and since that day I feel all evil
vanquished, my transgressions expiated.

A flame burns long; upon your roof
and mine, I saw the horror overflowing.
Young seedling, you sprouted; and in the cool
of truce I watched your plumage growing.

Kneeling I remain: the gift I dreamed
for all, not for me only, belongs to me
alone, God by man fractionated, by clotted blood
upon the topmost branch, upon the fruits.

ANNIVERSARIO

Dal tempo della tua nascita
sono in ginocchio, mia volpe.
È da quel giorno che sento
vinto il male, espiate le mie colpe.

Arse a lungo una vampa; sul tuo tetto,
sul mio, vidi l'orrore traboccare.
Giovane stelo tu crescevi; e io al rezzo
delle tregue spiavo il tuo piumare.

Resto in ginocchio: il dono che sognavo
non per me ma per tutti
appartiene a me solo, Dio diviso
dagli uomini, dal sangue raggrumato
sui rami alti, sui frutti.

DREAM OF THE PRISONER

Here, dawns and nights vary by few signs.

The zigzag of the starlings above the bell towers
on the days of conflict, my solitary wings,
a wisp of polar air,
the warden's eye at the peephole,
the cracking of crushed nuts, an oily
sputtering from the cellars, spits
actual or supposed—but the straw is golden
and the wine-like lantern is a hearth if, sleeping,
I believe myself extended at your feet.

The purge has always been, no reason.
He who abjures and who subscribes is said to save
himself from all this massacre of geese;
and he who groans, objures, confesses
and denounces, rules the roost,
rather than wind up in pâté
intended for the pestilential Gods.

Hesitant of thought, covered with wounds
from the thorny cot, I blended
with the flight of the moth powdered
by my sole upon the flagstone,
with the shifting kimonos of the lights
from massive towers mingling with the sunrise;
on the breeze I caught the burnt scent
of tea cakes in the ovens,
looking about, I embroidered rainbows

IL SOGNO DEL PRIGIONIERO

Albe e notti qui variano per pochi segni.

Lo zigzag degli storni sui battifredi
nei giorni di battaglia, mie sole ali,
un filo d'aria polare,
l'occhio del capoguardia dallo spioncino,
crac di noci schiacciate, un oleoso
sfrigolío dalle cave, girarrosti
veri o supposti—ma la paglia è oro,
la lanterna vinosa è focolare
se dormendo mi credo ai tuoi piedi.

La purga dura da sempre, senza un perché.
Dicono che chi abiura e sottoscrive
può salvarsi da questo sterminio d'oche;
che chi obiurga se stesso, ma tradisce
e vende carne d'altri, afferra il mestolo
anzi che terminare nel pâté
destinato agl'Iddii pestilenziali.

Tardo di mente, piagato
dal pungente giaciglio mi sono fuso
col volo della tarma che la mia suola
sfarina sull'impiantito,
coi kimoni cangianti delle luci
sciorinate all'aurora dai torrioni,
ho annusato nel vento il bruciaticcio
dei buccellati dai forni,
mi son guardato attorno, ho suscitato

243

on the horizons of the spiders' webs,
petals on the iron palisades;
I raised my self, relapsed in the abyss,
where century and minute are the same—

and the blows multiply, and the footsteps,
and still no inkling whether at the feast
I'll be the stuffer or the stuffed.
The waiting lasts a long time, my dream
of you has not yet found its end.

iridi su orizzonti di ragnateli
e petali sui tralicci delle inferriate,
mi sono alzato, sono ricaduto
nel fondo dove il secolo è il minuto—

e i colpi si ripentono ed i passi,
e ancora ignoro se sarò al festino
farcitore o farcito. L'attesa è lunga,
il mio sogno di te non è finito.

IN THE VOID
POINT COUNTERPOINT

IN THE VOID

The sun's mane was tangling
in the pickets of the orchard and on the beach
a few skiffs dawdled, half asleep.

The day gave out no sound
beneath the shining arc,
no pine cones
struck the ground, no bud
burst out behind the wall.

Silence engulfed everything,
our boat was moving still,
cutting a line upon the sand; a mark
long hanging high aloft, fell down.

Now the earth was an overflowing brim,
the tare was melted in the dazzling glare,
the flame became the froth upon the dark,
the breach widened and became too deep
for the anchor and for us
                    till all at once
a happening took place around us: the pearl valves
of the gulf swung closed, all and nothing went astray
and I awoke to the tones of your lip,
which had been mute—since then, captives
together in the vein which, all unseen
within the crystal, is waiting for its day.

NEL VUOTO

La criniera del sole s'invischiava
tra gli stecchi degli orti e sulla riva
qualche pigra scialuppa pareva assopita.

Non dava suono il giorno
sotto il lucido arco,
nè tonfava
pigna o sparava boccio
di là dai muri.

Il silenzio ingoiava tutto,
la nostra barca non s'era fermata,
tagliava a filo la sabbia, un segno a lungo
sospeso in alto precipitava.

Ora la terra era orlo che trabocca,
peso sciolto in barbaglio,
la vampa era la spuma dell'oscuro,
il fosso si allargava, troppo fondo
per l'àncora e per noi
             finché di scatto
qualcosa avvenne intorno, il vallo chiuse
le valve, nulla e tutto era perduto,
ed io fui desto al suono del tuo labbro
prima muto—da allora imprigionati
tutti e due nella vena che nel cristallo,
invisibile, attende la sua giornata.

POINT COUNTERPOINT

1

"Arsenio," she writes, "Asolando*
among my somber cypresses, I think
it would be time that we suspend suspension
of all worldly disappointments, as you
so ardently desired for me; time
to unfurl the sails and to suspend
the *epoché*.

"Don't say that the season is dark and even
the doves with tremulous wings have flown away south.
I am tired of living on memories.
Better the bite of hard frost than your torpor
of the somnambulist, or the lately wakened."

2

Hardly out of adolescence
I was tossed for half-a-life
into the Augean stables.

I didn't find two thousand steers, nor
did I ever notice animals;
but walking was poor along those corridors,
always more thickly littered with manure,
and it was hard to breathe; still, the human
bellowing increased from day to day.

BOTTA E RIPOSTA

1

« Arsenio » (lei mi scrive), « io qui asolante
tra i miei tetri cipressi penso che
sia ora di sospendere la tanto
da te per me voluta sospensione
d'ogni inganno mondano; che sia tempo
di spiegare le vele e di sospendere
l'epoché.

Non dire che la stagione è nera ed anche le tortore
con le tremule ali sono volate al sud.
Vivere di memorie non posso piú.
Meglio il morso del ghiaccio che il tuo torpore
di sonnambulo, o tardi risvegliato. »

2

Uscito appena dall'adolescenza
per metà della vita fui gettato
nelle stalle d'Augía.

Non vi trovai duemila bovi, né
mai vi scorsi animali;
pure nei corridoi, sempre piú folti
di letame, si camminava male,
e il respiro mancava; ma vi crescevano
di giorno in giorno i muggiti umani.

He was never to be seen;
however, the rabble waited for Him
for the present-arms: overflowing cornucopias,
forks and spits, a shish kabob
of fetid meat. And yet
no single time did He extend
a cloak's hem or the tapering of His crown
beyond the fecal ramparts made of ebony.

From year to year, then—and who could count
the seasons in that gloom?—some hand
which groped for unseen skylights
slipped its memento in: a lock
from Gerti, a cricket in a cage, last word
of Liuba's passage, the microfilm
of a euphuistic sonnet, sliding from
the fingers of the sleeping Clizia,
a clicking of wooden clogs (the crippled
housemaid from Monghidoro),
                    until from the crevasses
we were swept by the spray of the machine gun,
jaded ditch diggers caught bv mistake
by the custodians of the dunghills;

and finally, the crash: the incredible.

Lui non fu mai veduto.
La geldra però lo attendeva
per il presentat-arm: stracolmi imbuti,
forconi e spiedi, un'infilzata fetida
di saltimbocca. Eppure
non una volta Lui sporse
cocca di manto o punta di corona
oltre i bastioni d'ebano, fecali.

Poi d'anno in anno—e chi piú contava
le stagioni in quel buio?—qualche mano
che tentava invisibili spiragli
insinuò il suo memento: un ricciolo
di Gerti, un grillo in gabbia, ultima traccia
del transito di Liuba, il microfilm
d'un sonetto eufuìsta scivolato
dalle dita di Clizia addormentata,
un ticchettio di zoccoli (la serva
zoppa di Monghidoro)
                        finché dai cretti
il ventaglio di un mitra ci ributtava,
badilanti infiacchiti colti in fallo
dai bargelli del brago.

Ed infine fu il tonfo: l'incredibile.

To liberate us, to seal off the tangled
guts within a lake, an instant was enough
for the riled Alpheus. By that time,
who waited for it? What difference
could a new swamp make? Or breathing
other similar emanations? Or soaring
over rafts of excrement? And could it be a sun,
that filthy bait, sweat from chimneys
on the roofs; could they be men,
real; living men,
these giant ants from off the docks?

. . .

        (I wonder
if you still will read me. But now at least
you know all about me, my prison and my later life.
You know that the eagle is not fathered
by the rat.)

* On October 15, 1889, Robert Browning wrote to Mrs.
Arthur Bronson from the northern Italian town of Asolo
concerning his volume, Asolando: Fancies and Facts
(London: Smith, Elder & Co., 1890): "I unite, you will
see, the disconnected poems by a title-name popularly
ascribed to the inventiveness of the ancient secretary
of Queen Cornaro whose palace tower still overlooks us:
Asolare—to disport in the open air, amuse oneself at
random.' "

A liberarci, a chiuder gli intricati
cunicoli in un lago, bastò un attimo
allo stravolto Alfeo. Chi l'attendeva
ormai? Che senso aveva quella nuova
palta? e il respirare altre ed eguali
zaffate? e il vorticare sopra zattere
di sterco? ed era sole quella sudicia
esca di scolaticcio sui fumaioli,
erano uomini forse,
veri uomini vivi
i formiconi degli approdi?

. . .

       (Penso
che forse non mi leggi piú. Ma ora
tu sai tutto di me,
della mia prigionia e del mio dopo;
ora sai che non può nascere l'aquila
dal topo.)